caught

What are People Saying About

caught

We endorse any couple who is willing and courageous enough to tell their own story for the public. Our culture needs more of this kind of honesty. Robbie and John Iobst have done this very thing in *Caught*.

—**Mark Laaser, M.Div., Ph.D.**, Director of Faithful and True, Christian counseling center, Specializing in the treatment of individuals and couples struggling with sexual purity/infidelity and relational betrayal.

Robbie and John have written a raw, honest and amazingly helpful treatise on a topic most of us are embarrassed to discuss: sexual addiction. This addiction has both publicly and privately destroyed marriages, lives and ministries; yet most of the devoted men and women of God I've known in my 30+ years of ministry have no solutions. We offer lame guidance or, as one young wife told her husband in a counseling session, "Just stop that!". I'm ashamed of the numbers of men that I've abandoned to figure their own way out of this horrible demonic entity called pornography, all because I had no genuine or real answers or solutions. I'm so thankful for the Iobst's honesty and vulnerability in *Caught*. I'm so pleased to finally have a practical and real answer for the 7 out of 10 men I see weekly who are captives to pornography.

—**Phil Floyd**, Director of Caleb's Hearts Ministries

The longer I live, the more I fall head-over-heels-in-love with three things: A good story, an honest friend, and unfailing grace. *Caught* accomplishes all three at once. To those living in an undone life as a result of sexual addiction, you will find hope and the first steps toward healing right here. There's a Savior ready to catch you. Let Him, my friend. Let Him.

—**Michele Cushatt**, author of
Undone: A Story of Making Peace With An Unexpected Life

Caught is the honest saga of two broken people struggling to make a marriage whole. For anyone who has struggled with addiction, you will see yourself in John and Robbie. Filled with honest struggles and hard-won hope, this is a book worthy of your time and attention.

—**Kathi Lipp**, author of *The Husband Project*

Caught is raw, real and full of redemption. John & Robbie are brutally honest about a topic that is often taboo. I admire their courage to speak about pornography addiction in order to help other marriages heal. They teach us how to take a marriage between two imperfect people dealing with expectations, insecurities and addiction and find hope in JESUS.

—**Angie Austin**, host of the nationally syndicated show,
Daybreak USA and *The Good News With Angie Austin*

caught

*In Denial, In the Act, &
In the Arms of a Loving God*

a Story *of a* Marriage Lost
and a Marriage Redeemed

John & Robbie
IOBST

New York

caught

In Denial, In the Act, & In the Arms of a Loving God:
a Story of a Marriage Lost and a Marriage Redeemed

Published in New York, New York, by Morgan James Publishing. Morgan James and The Entrepreneurial Publisher are trademarks of Morgan James, LLC. www.MorganJamesPublishing.com

The Morgan James Speakers Group can bring authors to your live event. For more information or to book an event visit The Morgan James Speakers Group at www.TheMorganJamesSpeakersGroup.com.

All Scripture is taken from the New International Version Bible.

Shelfie

A **free** eBook edition is available with the purchase of this print book.

CLEARLY PRINT YOUR NAME ABOVE IN UPPER CASE

Instructions to claim your free eBook edition:
1. Download the Shelfie app for Android or iOS
2. Write your name in **UPPER CASE** above
3. Use the Shelfie app to submit a photo
4. Download your eBook to any device

ISBN 978-1-63047-973-2 paperback
ISBN 978-1-63047-974-9 eBook
ISBN 978-1-63047-975-6 hardcover
Library of Congress Control Number: 2016902180

Cover Design by:
Rachel Lopez
www.r2cdesign.com

Interior Design by:
Bonnie Bushman
The Whole Caboodle Graphic Design

In an effort to support local communities and raise awareness and funds, Morgan James Publishing donates a percentage of all book sales for the life of each book to Habitat for Humanity Peninsula and Greater Williamsburg.

Get involved today, visit
www.MorganJamesBuilds.com

Habitat for Humanity® Peninsula and Greater Williamsburg Building Partner

Dedicated to Doug Zabriskie, Betty Gazaway,
and Theresa and Jeff Hornbuckle.
Thank you for believing in a future we couldn't see.

Table of Contents

Foreword

John and Robbie Iobst are inspirations to me, as people who started out in the slimy pit, and who have allowed God to break them of their denial, heal them of their shame, and take them into the light to a new and better life of freedom from bondage.

They now are able to take what they have learned, and bring a message and a process of recovery to others who desperately need it.

I was privileged to have participated in their healing into a new life of honesty, genuineness and appropriate transparency. Both of them had been subject to addictions: John to lust and sexual compulsivity, and Robbie to the "I will be perfectly all right when I fix him" disease. Both of them are and were sincere Christians, who overly spiritualized their emotional/relational problems, and who hid in church leadership positions.

There is a lot of hiding in our churches, even among church leaders. I thank Jesus that He is bringing our performance-based religious practices to an end by showering us with the unconditional love of our Father in Heaven, and His family. In doing this, He is freeing us up to be able to admit that we may have serious problems, and that as we admit them and receive help, we can be cleansed and healed.

I am thoroughly convinced that just as "all things work together for good for those who love Him and are called according to His purposes", that He uses addiction and recovery to bring us to an acceptance of our brokenness, a need for His unconditional love, and the love of others who are also on the journey of recovery.

John and Robbie understand now that this is not just a spiritual problem, and we need more than spiritual answers. Just as a man with a broken leg needs prayer *and* a doctor, addicts need more than just prayer and a few well-selected Biblical platitudes. John and Robbie prayed, went to and led groups and Bible studies, pleaded with God, made declarations, swore on their Bibles, and more, and they continued in their broken darkness.

Now they understand that addiction is a brain and relational/attachment disorder. It involves emotional, spiritual, physical and cognitive components. It is chronic, progressive, and is sooner or later terminal, if not arrested.

When Robbie declared "I won't live this way anymore. That's it. I have had enough, we need to get help.", and she meant it, John got help purely and simply because he didn't want to lose his Higher Power — Robbie. Then he started to learn and accept that recovery was for him first. Then Robbie went deeper into her voyage of personal acceptance, vulnerability, and healing.

This book is a splendid story of two people who are learning that they are human beings, and not human doings. It is an inspiring and open look into their private lives, their problems and weaknesses, as well as their victories, growth and healing. They had to first become people who knew and loved themselves as Christ does, before they could truly love and bless each other unconditionally, while remaining true to themselves.

It is also a "how to" manual, with explicit, clear, concise directions on a new way of life that works for them. They have gleaned Biblical wisdom, Holy Spirit truth, and the wisdom passed down through generations of people in addictive recovery.

If you, or someone you know, may be involved in sexual brokenness and addiction, this book is a valuable resource and tool.

Doug Zabriskie is a Licensed Marriage and Family Therapist who has operated a San Diego private practice since 1991. He has specialized in treating hundreds of sexually addicted men, as well as their spouses/partners and families.

He partners with therapists at Balance Mental Health and Wellness Center to provide a comprehensive recovery and healing program which promotes emotional, relational, spiritual and sexual health, and not just addictive abstinence.

Acknowledgements

This book has been a very long process and we have a tremendous community of support that have helped us along the way.

Thank you:

Noah, Hannah, Sarah and Marriah. We have the four best offspring in the world and this book would not exist without your permission. We love each of you very, very much.

Lucy and Nan Iobst, Karen and Paul Pratt, Perry and Kasey Floyd. Family support is everything and you have each cheered us on in this process.

Phil and Lory Floyd. So many times you have prayed for us, dreamed with us, counseled us and yelled louder than most, "Do it!" Thank you both for such wonderful friendship and support. And we just happen to be related.

Teal Elliott. Thank you for editing our book. When Robbie discovered that your life verse was 1 Corinthians 14:40, her heart did a little flip flop. God gave us a great assistant and friend. You and Carl have been such blessings.

Kim Stewart, AnneMarie Stone and Margaret Youssef. We are immensely grateful to you for being our first readers and giving us invaluable corrections and suggestions.

Everyone at Morgan James Publishing. Your professional attitude mixed with a real caring for excellence and ministry has proven to be invaluable to us.

Our San Diego community who stood by us and loved us through a really difficult time. Joani, Mark, Theresa, Jeff, Desha, Linda, Susy, Stacey and Lan, our home group and recovery groups. Community makes it all happen.

Our prayer team of Ron, Roberta, Jeff, Annie, Sherry, Scott, Tony, Melody, Phil, Lory, Chuck, Leslie, Dianne and Rich. Writing a book about some of the most painful times in our marriage is difficult to say the least and would not have been possible without a dedicated team of faithful people praying for us every step of the way.

Pastor Anthony Pranno and our friends at Rocky Mountain Community Church. We are so blessed to have a family in Christ like you.

Robbie:

Michele Cushatt, Kay Day, Stacy Voss and Dianne Daniels. You, my fellow writers and friends kept me sane through this, while also correcting grammar. I love you ladies!

Sherry Johnson, Lisa Vanderley. Thank you for the 6am Egg and I breakfasts. To have a place where I could cry with Jesus girls while eating great food is such a blessing.

Rebecca Barth and Lisa Nickerson. Nothing is better than having two new sisters who always point me to Jesus. Thank you both so much.

John. Watching you transform in God's hands has blessed me so much. Thank you for putting me first over and over again and making our marriage the priority. I love you.

John:

Aaron Vinyard. You are my brother from another mother who has been a deep and constant support in my recovery and writing this book.

Recovery brothers, for whom I can never be sufficiently grateful. No book about recovery would be possible without recovery and my recovery would not be possible without these men who by tradition must remain anonymous. You know who you are.

My Band of Brothers (BOB): J and Daniel. You regularly point my wandering heart back to Jesus and have provided practical support all along the way.

My Big Ass BOB: Chuck, Dennis, Jim, Mark, Scott, Tony and Tony. You walked with me before this book was even a consideration and you were part of the process all along the way.

Robbie. You had the courage to trust Jesus and stay in this marriage when there were no signs of hope. You later had the courage to walk back into our darkest days together and put it down on paper. I love you and I pray that this book is a blessing to your heart.

Finally, we both want to thank the Redeemer of broken marriages and lost hearts, Jesus. Without the love and forgiveness of God, this book would simply not be.

Introduction

At the age of eight in Los Angeles, California John saw pornography for the first time.

At the age of eight in Van Horn, Texas Robbie saw pornography for the first time.

Years later, we got married and hoped to live happily ever after. That didn't happen. Pornography and its effects would follow us and attempt to ravage our marriage and our family. Pornography masks itself as an innocuous activity, an expected part of growing up and an aid to marital bliss.

Lies.

Pornography is a vicious killer.

This is a story of hope. God is a rescuer and a relentless pursuer of our hearts. He rescued us. He can rescue you, too.

"(Jesus) who gave himself for us to redeem us from all wickedness and to purify for himself a people that are his very own, eager to do what is good"
(Titus 2:14).

Section One:

CAUGHT IN DENIAL

"His talk is smooth as butter, yet war is in his heart; his words are more soothing than oil, yet they are drawn swords"
(Psalm 55:21).

Chapter One

Happily Ever After?

But those aren't always the best tales to hear,
though they may be the best tales to get landed in!
I wonder what sort of a tale we've fallen into?
—J.R.R. Tolkien[1]

Robbie:

Once upon a time...

"I've found your husband!" My friend Lela, short and sassy with short and sassy hair, smiled as if she'd caught an elusive and rare bird she wanted to show me.

"Thank you Lela, but no thank you."

"Just meet him, Robbie." Her mischievous smile was difficult to resist. But I managed. "No, Lela. No."

We had the same exchange about once a month for the next year. Little did I know, she was having the same conversation with John.

"John, she works at my school. You're going to love her."

"No, Lela."

"But John, listen…"

"No."

In early January of 1996, Lela caught us both worn down the same week. "So you'll come to my house for dinner and meet him, Robbie?"

"If I do will you never bring this up again?"

"Absolutely."

"John, you'll come? Maybe you can cook part of the meal?"

"Fine. I'll do this. But from now on, leave my dating life alone."

On the day of our blind date, I attended a wedding for a fellow teacher. At the reception, I sat with a group of my drama students. When time came for the throwing of the bouquet, I gave my food a hundred percent of my attention, hoping no one would notice I was not going to participate. My students noticed.

"Miss Floyd, get out there. You could catch the bouquet."

I played with the cake on my plate. "No, I think it is a silly tradition. I'll go out there and get an elbow in the face by a girl desperate to catch a bunch of flowers that will not lead to anything."

Joey, one of my favorite students asked, "Don't you hope to get married?"

"No, I think I am all out of hope, Joey." At 33, I didn't think it was ever going to happen.

Joey grinned. "Miss Floyd, you hope and we will pray."

That night, Lela's stubborn streak won a victory, and I went to her house for dinner. When I walked into the kitchen, I saw John stirring broccoli and beef in a wok.

"He cooks, Robbie." Lela said with an annoying smile. "We know you don't."

Her husband laughed, and I curtly said, "Thanks Lela."

John introduced himself, and we all began the fingers-on-the-chalkboard ritual of small talk. During the conversation, I asked God to help me relax and be pleasant to this man, even though I knew it would go nowhere. John possessed very kind eyes and was indeed tall, dark and handsome but I wasn't feeling anything. And why would I give Lela the satisfaction? I was finally accepting that life without being a Mrs. would not be equal to waterboarding.

Maybe.

After dinner, we played a board game that resembled charades. By this time, I was beat and ready to go home.

But then the word given to act out was "carpet." This was one of those moments that changed my life.

Lela got the word, and she yelled out "carpet!"

Then I said for absolutely no reason, "You don't want a carpet..."

And John and I simultaneously called out, "You want an A-R-E-A rug," saying the word area with the exact same exaggerated accent. We were both imitating a line from an obscure Tom Hanks movie called *Punchline.*[2]

I looked at this man in shock. We both laughed. "John, you've seen that movie?"

"I loved that movie." He grinned.

My heart did an actual, no fooling, honest to goodness flip flop. I didn't hear wedding bells or see my name Mrs. John Iobst written in the sky. It wasn't a moment like many moments in the past where I would meet someone and immediately start planning the wedding.

My friends, other single women in their early thirties joined me in that quest. We were all hunters, seeking out the perfect prey. Sometimes we jumped the gun. Maybe often. We had a catch-phrase among ourselves. "Hi—it's not just a greeting, it's a commitment."

This wasn't like that. John Iobst piqued my interest. In that moment, I discovered a wonderful possibility. Kind of like seeing the perfect royal blue dress in a shop in your size and your price range. Fantastic - but you still have to try it on. He had potential.

The next week he sent yellow roses (my favorite) to the high school where I taught and attached a note that said, "Academy Award Winner for Best First Date." He didn't know it at the time, but I am a huge fan of the Academy Awards. I was in "twitterpation," like Thumper in *Bambi*.[3] When he asked me out for a second date, my answer was immediate. Yes.

It felt like a fairy tale. A wonderful, finally I've-met-my-prince, fairy tale. I'd prayed for a Godly man to whisk me off my feet all of my life. Here he was! We were Sleeping Beauty and Prince Charming.

Okay, maybe Fiona and Shrek, but still, it was a fairy tale. We'd live happily ever after.

John:

But storybook romances and romantic comedies never show the entire truth. And for both Robbie and I, the truth was not as pretty as a Disney story. When I met Robbie I wasn't looking for a relationship at all. I was appeasing Lela to get her off my back.

But then.

Robbie's personality, character and sense of humor captivated me, and I was the one swept off my feet. I didn't know what kind of future we could have, but I knew I wanted to spend more time with this amazing woman to see what was possible.

On our second date we saw *Mr. Holland's Opus*,[4] a super sentimental film we both enjoyed. After it ended, we went to an Italian restaurant and shut it down talking. We had no idea we'd talked for so long until we noticed all the tables around us had chairs on top of them, and a waiter was mopping the floor. It was like a scene from a movie.

The future looked good.

Now the problem was I didn't know if I was good enough for her. While I would call myself a Christian, I didn't consider myself a Godly man. In fact, if I'd done the honorable thing it would have been to never see Robbie again. But my selfishness kicked in and I wanted more, so I started pretending to be what I thought she wanted me to be.

Robbie:

My quest—it became a quest in every sense—to find a Godly man and marry him started in junior high shortly after I asked Jesus Christ to be the Lord, the Master, and the Guide of my life. As the hormones began their dance in my body, I found that the opposite sex looked quite appealing. I wasn't just playing the game of elementary boyfriend/girlfriend. I truly believed that finding a boyfriend meant that I belonged. I fit in with everyone else.

At first my attractions were limited to those wonderful Osmond boys, mainly Donny. Posters from the magazine *16* adorned my walls. I knew in my heart that it was possible for Donny Osmond to come to my small town in Texas and fall in love with me.

Someone in my church explained to me that Donny Osmond was a Mormon. What is a Mormon? This simple question opened the door for the teaching of unequally-yoked dating. I was disappointed to say the least. But soon my fantasies were tailored to meet my standards of religion. Okay, I would witness to Donny and he would become a Christian and then we would get married.

The belief that I was to marry a Godly man developed into a foundational doctrine for the way I lived. To be complete was to be loved by a man who served Jesus. In my early 20's I was rejected by someone I thought I would marry. I began gaining weight. By the time I met John, I was very heavy with a heavy heart. In desperate attempts to be loved, I'd been rejected many times. My biggest fear as I got to know John was that he, too, would reject me. I couldn't let that happen. We were two people who each brought a U haul of baggage with us. That baggage drew us to one another in an ironic way. I became very comfortable in hiding my insecurities and fears.

John:

I also became comfortable in hiding from Robbie who I truly was. It was a match made in—heaven? I was excited to introduce Robbie to my three daughters. They visited on weekends and so on a Saturday night, I invited Robbie to my house to have dinner with us.

Robbie:

Terror could be easily defined as the act of meeting the daughters of the man you are thinking about marrying. Even though I was a high school teacher and I loved kids, I had no idea how to act. I tried to be myself, but fear clouded every movement. The night I met Marriah, Sarah and Hannah was one of the most significant nights of my life. Yet I didn't understand at all how important these girls were going to be to me. In fact, my mind and heart were so filled with blind love for John that I didn't try to get to know them. I just wanted them to like me, because John was their dad.

That dinner gave me a glimpse of the three beautiful women that would eventually become a part of my heart. While we were eating dinner, Sarah, the middle girl, excused herself to use the restroom. She was eleven at the time.

From the restroom she called out, "Daddy, I need toilet paper."

John called back, "It's under the sink."

A few minutes later Sarah came back to the table and announced, "I couldn't find the toilet paper so I used the towel."

I was flabbergasted. What kind of girls were these?

And then they laughed. She was kidding. At eleven, her sense of humor was already wickedly sarcastic, like her dad. Marriah and Hannah proved to be just as quick-witted. Three of the best gifts I've received in marrying John were these three, now grown, ladies who have given me my grand-girls.

Despite these beautiful bright spots, John and I continued to lie to each other about our hearts. We didn't only put on our best faces; we also hid the ugliness that lived in us both. The unpleasant truth that would appear after we got married.

The following is a summary of actual conversations during our dating. In italics is what we were *really* thinking:

Robbie: Great movie.

John: I thought so, too.

Robbie: I saw you tear up there.

John: Yep, I almost cried like a little girl. But I thought on our second date it wouldn't look good.

I must impress her. I can't believe I almost cried. Where is my man card?

Robbie: (Laughs) I love that you cried. My dad cries at movies.

He must be extremely sensitive. I like that.

John: Tell me about yourself.

Robbie: I grew up in Texas…

Robbie, give him your resume of Godly acts and character. Be funny but not too funny. Smart but not too smart. I want him to like me and sometimes, I can be too much. Too loud. Too everything. And whatever you do, don't eat much.

Robbie: What about you?

John: I was born in Florida…

John, give her your best nice guy version of your story. I want to impress her, but maybe I should just tell her all the horrible details and get the rejection out of the way. Well, not all the details.

Robbie: So you're divorced?

John: Yes.

Robbie: But you were a pastor for a while?

John: Yes.

Robbie: Cool.

Divorced? Oh well, that doesn't matter. I've hit the jackpot! I dreamed and prayed for a Godly man. To be a pastor's wife is the ultimate prize. And he used to be a pastor. I have won the man lottery. But he could still reject me. I am fat and even though I don't eat much around him, I still eat plenty at home.

John: So never married?

Robbie: No.

John: Engaged?

Robbie: No.

John: Okay.

She's not running away from me. I like her. When should I tell her about my "struggle?"

John: Robbie, I need to tell you something. I was a sex addict.

Robbie: Are you better?

What's a sex addict? Does that mean he loves sex too much? I don't want to know. I'm a virgin and I don't want to talk about that. As long as he's better.

John: Oh, absolutely. I am much better.

I'm better at hiding it.

Robbie: Do you want to pray?

It is important that I marry my spiritual leader.

John: Um…you go ahead.

What? Pray? Uh-oh.

Robbie: Okay.

Maybe he is just shy about praying. This is a red flag, Robbie. But it doesn't matter. He was a pastor. He can pray. I am looking for a Godly, spiritual leader. He says he's a Christian, and I am looking for a Godly man. So what if he doesn't want to pray? He is a Christian and he won't reject me.

Robbie: John, I need to say something and you may think it's weird.

John: Okay.

Robbie: I am fat. You can see that, right?

I might as well get the rejection out of the way. He can't find me attractive, can he? It isn't possible so why put myself through the pain of rejection again?

John: You are beautiful.

Robbie: Really?

Is he for real? He won't reject me?

John: You are beautiful and I don't charity date. I want a woman with character and you have tremendous character.

I'm not looking for character; I'm looking for someone who won't notice mine.

We both decided to take it slow.

So of course, five months after that initial blind date at Lela's house, our fairy tale took another turn. We got married on June 22, 1996 and began our love story.

Was it happily ever after?

We had no idea of the pain to come.

Chapter Two

Fairy Tale Wounds

Our deepest wounds surround our greatest gifts.
—Ken Page[5]

John:

"Dad, I have big news."

I was training to become a pastor when I called my father to tell him. I hoped that he would be proud of me. He never married my mother, and I only spent three days with him after I met him at age nineteen. But I still wanted his approval. I needed his love.

I told him in excitement and pride.

He said, "You'll be good at that, John; you come from a long line of conmen."

His words became my "father wound" as John Eldridge describes in his book, *Wild at Heart*.[6] That wound turned into the belief that I brought nothing good or true to any situation. My father's words had to be true, right? He's my father. I'm nothing more than a liar and a conman. Because of this wound, I resolved to never let anyone, even Robbie, count on me.

Most wounds don't leave visible scars. My father's curse cut me deeply, but it was an easily hidden wound. "If you really knew me you would reject me," became my core belief. So my wounding kept me from opening up to anyone.

After our wedding, Robbie and I flew to Jackson Hole, Wyoming for our honeymoon. A friend gave us a week at a beautiful cabin just outside of town in a mountain setting. We were ready to begin our lives having fun and laughing. Robbie was the youngest of four and I was an only child (with lots of half brothers and sisters.) Our birth order and temperaments contributed to our personalities. We knew how to have a good time.

However, I brought several wounds in my luggage, not just my "father wound". This was my second marriage and my first marriage failed in large part because of my addiction. So I brought the fear of rejection. I took that wound and decided to hide that broken part of my heart from Robbie, too. The less she knew about my addiction, the safer I would be.

And packed in my overnight bag with my shaving kit and toothbrush, I squeezed in the wound of being "nice." I was a nice guy, never rocking anyone's boat. This wound taught me to never share my true self to Robbie. Not on our honeymoon and not in our marriage.

Robbie:

I brought my own wound into our marriage. As we entered the life of being Mr. and Mrs. John Iobst, I carried in my purse the lie/wound that I would never be good enough to be loved — truly loved. The wound came when I was eight years old.

Remember giving out pictures in elementary school? It was a big deal when I was little. In third grade, I was in Mr. Brown's class. One day he announced that at the end of the next day, we would exchange pictures in class. I went home and cut out my pictures and started writing notes on the back.

Maria, you are a good friend and funny. Stay cool. Robbie
Pam, thanks for being so smart. Don't ever change. Robbie

The most important note I wrote was for Cecil B. McDougal. (I've changed his name.) I loved Cecil. He was funny, cute, and athletic. And he was in Mr. Brown's class, too. I really wanted him to "like – like" me, as a girlfriend. So I wrote *Cecil, you are a great guy. Robbie*

Calling someone a great guy in third grade is basically telling them you love them and want to have their babies. I was ready to be Cecil's wife.

At the end of the next day, we walked around the class exchanging photos. I gathered up all my courage and walked to Cecil's desk where he was sitting.

"I have a picture for you, Cecil."

He answered immediately, "Okay, I'll give you one too." He took a moment and signed the back of his picture and handed it to me. I was so excited. I decided to read his words on my walk home. I would be alone when I read, *Robbie I like you. Do you like me? Check the box yes or no.*

About half way to my home on Summer Street was a large piece of land covered in greasewood and creosote bushes. In the middle of the brush, I stopped and took a deep breath. I read:

Robbie,
You are a nice girl who will get a boyfriend when you lose weight.
Cecil

What?

My heart broke. The enemy shot a flaming arrow and it hit my heart, wounding me. I don't blame Cecil. He was just a kid going through who knows what. Maybe his father talked about his mother's weight often. But the wound took hold, and I believed his words.

The same year I was in my parent's bathroom, and I picked up a magazine. Inside its pages, I saw pornography. The enemy continued to attack my heart. Did I have to look like *that* woman, and do what *that* woman was doing to be loved?

Two years later, I gave my Dad a picture of me. Recently, I found it and on the back I'd written, *Daddy, you are a great dad. I'm sorry I'm so ugly.*

The wound became my identity. Along with it came the lies society and movies perpetuate. I expected our honeymoon to be perfection, Eden-like, with slow motion scenes where John and I ran into each other's arms. A real life fairy tale. I assumed that our honeymoon would be full of romantic love and sex. Lots of sex. This did not happen on our honeymoon.

I was a virgin and he was a sex addict, so I thought we would have sex all the time. That's what the movies depicted. But we didn't. Maybe he loved sex, but not sex with me. I was fat, right? I wasn't worth loving, until I lost weight and looked like *that* woman.

Deep in my heart I thought marrying John would heal me. I was finally completely loved. But it didn't work that way. The wound and my feelings of inadequacy stayed cemented in my heart.

John:

As soon as we were on our honeymoon, I felt like I was walking on egg shells, like I needed to be extra careful not to say or do anything that would make Robbie feel insecure or unloved. Nothing seemed to work. If we were sexual, she was upset that we weren't talking more. If we did anything else, it seemed she was upset because I didn't want her or we weren't haven't sex. I couldn't win. Our honeymoon was near Yellowstone Park, and we drove there one day. Robbie spent much of the time sleeping in the car. I felt like I was wrong for suggesting we go to the park. When we visited a park gift shop, Robbie wanted to buy something so we could "commemorate" the visit. I didn't want to spend too much money, so I felt like the bad guy again. This was our honeymoon – a time to celebrate our love – but I felt like I was doing it wrong. I believed I was a huge disappointment to Robbie. In my crazy mind (it's like a bad neighborhood at night—don't go there alone) I figured Robbie was already looking for a way out of our marriage.

My only option was to push all those thoughts down and pretend everything was "nice" and "fine." I defended myself by acting as if Robbie's expectations were silly or unreasonable. The truth was I couldn't face not being enough for her. The fear haunted me that she was going to leave me, and I would be a twice-divorced middle aged man.

We had a great time in Jackson Hole, covering up the reality of our hearts with laughter and fun events. We could talk about anything, if it had a punchline. Our wounds weren't funny, but they travelled with us.

From the beginning, our wounds *ran* our marriage.

The enemy would use them to *ruin* our marriage.

Chapter Three

The Rules of Denial

Denial ain't just a river in Egypt.
—Anonymous[7]

Robbie:

My definition of the term "helpmate" when I got married:

> *Noun — a wife who helps her husband*
> *become everything she wants him to be.*

John did not have the same definition. In fact, he actually refused my advice. Some might call it control, but I knew what was best. Wasn't this in the vows?

He didn't always act as I thought he should. He wasn't as socially acceptable as I thought he should be. Being the Godly woman I was, I would become his "helpmate" and instruct him on what was appropriate and what was not. I began to judge him for being who he was.

I did my best to mold him into the perfect husband. He was not having any of it. I realized it might be a more difficult task than I imagined, but I was determined to "fix" him.

John:

With every piece of "helpful" advice Robbie offered me, my resentment grew. I had been attracted to her confident way of talking to everyone. But now, I discovered a control freak living in our home. Apparently, I did not live according to her standards.

She used to love my humor no matter where we were. During our first few years of marriage she only enjoyed it when we were at home. It was like she wanted me to be one version of John outside the home and the other version inside the home. This made for a lot of confusion and resentment. I wasn't going to change because she wanted it. Who did she think she was, the boss of me?

Robbie:

I was the boss of him.

I was raised in Texas by a mother who loved us and raised us according to the old-fashioned view that you keep private things private. "Robbie, you don't need to tell everything you know" was a common phrase. Keeping family stuff at home was the rule. Not that we had great secrets in our family like abuse or a war criminal kept in the closet. It was just embedded in me that I needed to act one way in public and the other way in private. This was done subtly, not like I wore a big mask in public.

I learned this behavior by watching my mother. She loved bridge and had a bridge club of women over to our house every few months.

My mother was not a slob or a hoarder at all, but she wasn't a neat freak either. If you came over to the house, you'd see our home was comfortable, lived in. However, when the bridge club was coming it was a different story.

Mama turned into a sergeant and we, her privates with dust rags and a mop. We had tile that had grooves in it and before the bridge women descended on our home, we would sit on the floor, pairing knives in hand, and scrape out every little groove. Many, if not all women clean their house before company comes. But the stark difference between Mama in an easy going kind-of-messy home and Sergeant Mama made the concept of public versus private a way of life for me.

When I heard Miranda Lambert's song "Mama's Broken Heart" I called my sister Karen.

She agreed that the song lyrics were very close to how we were raised. Phrases like:

"Run and hide your crazy and start actin like a lady

Cause I raised you better, gotta keep it together

Even when you fall apart."[8]

So when I got married to John, I brought this philosophy into our home. John needed to be smooth, popular and well, like *me*, when he was in public. I didn't care if he was goofy in private.

John:

Possibly the first time in my life that I heard the term "public versus private" was early in our marriage. I don't remember what I said or did, but I do recall being scolded for saying or doing something in front of other people (public) that offended Robbie's sensibilities. That same behavior would not have so much as raised an eyebrow if we were alone (private). I was confused by this but was strongly encouraged to adopt this form of behavior modification.

I found it silly. After all, we are who we are, and we should be who we are wherever we are. Isn't that the definition of integrity? In my pride and arrogance,

I decided Robbie was just wrong about this and that my "transparent" approach to living was emotionally, relationally and spiritually superior in every way. That was all the excuse I needed to not change a thing. Clearly, I had the moral high ground.

Ironically, I had my own version of public versus private. But mine was "public versus never share with anyone in any circumstance". It was a shame management solution; simply keep hidden the parts of me that were shameful.

She was wrong, and I was right. I had the right to keep secrets from my wife. At the same time, I openly mocked her for wanting to keep secrets in the family rather than sharing them publicly.

Robbie:

I also wanted John to be humble, like a Godly man is supposed to be. Instead, I observed him being what I thought was prideful. And in public, no less. I tried to explain to him that he needed to work on this behavior. In public, I wanted us to shine as a Godly man and woman and he, again, was not being who I thought he should be.

John:

This public versus private philosophy ushered in a great covering of denial into our home. I lived in denial of needing help for my secret addiction. Robbie lived in denial by refusing to accept me for who I was and by telling the world that I was this Godly man (one she had concocted in her head in junior high school.)

Our two incompatible versions of public versus private behavior became the norm in our family. We lived in two separate worlds of denial. In essence, we refused to live in the truth of who we were and who God made us to be.

Robbie:

Without realizing it, we were sliding into the worst kind of abyss—a marriage of lies. An impasse of denial. War was declared.

Cold, bitter, silent war.

Chapter Four

The Cold War in our Home

"Cold war" according to www.thefreedictionary.com

1. A state of political tension and military rivalry between nations that stops short of full scale war, especially that which existed between the United States and the Soviet Union following World War II

2. A state of rivalry and tension between two factions, groups or individuals that stops short of open, violent confrontation. [9]

Robbie:

Lady Astor famously said to Winston Churchill, "If you were my husband, I'd poison your brandy." Churchill replied. "If you were my wife I'd drink it."[10]

This reminds me of the cold war in our home. We were at a stalemate, angry at each other most of the time, while pretending we were happily married. It is a horrible state to live in your haven with your mate and feel alone. We both felt this way because we isolated our hearts.

Lines were drawn.

I wanted John to behave in public like me. John wanted me to get over my hypocrisy.

I wanted John and me to resolve all of our differences quickly. John wanted to have time to process.

I wanted John to *feel* the way I did. If I was excited, he needed to be excited. John wanted to feel the way he felt and not be controlled by me.

I wanted John to talk about his feelings. John wanted to answer everything in one word.

We were in a cold war.

John:

I was right. She was wrong. Pretty obvious to me.

Robbie:

The final conflict in our cold war was the most pervasive in our home—pornography.

In an article entitled "When Children View Pornography" Rob Jackson wrote,

Pornography is propaganda and generates destructive myths about sexuality. Once exposed, it will be critically important that a comprehensive sex education gets underway, if it has not already been initiated. The child will need to learn what and how to think about sexuality. More than mere behaviors, parents will want to communicate the core values of sexuality, the multifaceted risks of sex outside of marriage, and their ongoing compassion for what it must be like to grow up in this culture.[11]

When I saw that picture in the magazine in my father's bathroom, I never told anyone, especially my parents, about what I'd seen. I didn't get to "debrief" about this depiction of sex. I wasn't educated about sex. My parents would later teach me morals concerning sex, but they never prayed over me. They never engaged in spiritual warfare for their daughter.

I believe with all of my heart that pornography is a living, breathing demon. That might sound a bit radical, but when this spirit lived in my home, my marriage and my life was almost destroyed. Prayer over my heart and what I'd seen would've combatted this spirit when I was young and helped me when I grew up.

By being exposed to pornography at such an early age, it was like I was introduced to this evil spirit. Now in young boys like John, this might lead to a skewed view of sexuality and problems with lust. For me, meeting this evil spirit opened the door to attacks on my identity. That picture led me to believe that women must look like the woman in that photograph. Since I was a child when I first saw it, I hadn't developed a shield of faith to protect my heart from the flaming arrows of the enemy. My parents didn't have the wherewithal to use their shields for me in prayer and healthy discussions.

By the time I met John, I'd seen pornography several times. I'd acted out rarely, and when I did I felt horrible guilt. When I married John, I assumed my dealings with pornography was over.

The first time I found pornography in our home, it jarred me. What? We were married. How could he look at this?

John:

We then had the same conversation that we would have many times, each after Robbie found pornography in our house:

> Robbie: John, what are you doing?
> Me: I'm sorry.
> Robbie: We're Christians! We don't do this!

Me: I know.

Robbie: You can't do this. You cannot look at this kind of thing.

Me: (Hanging my head in shame.) I know. I'll stop doing it.

Robbie: You better.

It always happened again. Robbie tried shaming me into stopping and it always worked. For a day.

After years of living in the cold war and finding evidence of my addiction several times, Robbie told me we needed to see someone. She thought that would fix me. That's when we went to see Doug, a Christian counselor.

Robbie:

Doug Zabriskie entered our life. He is a tall, lanky Christian counselor with a cowboy grin and laid back style that John and I both found we liked. When we met him, I sensed he would side with me. It would be simple really. I needed validation. John needed fixing.

To my delight, Doug agreed with me. But then he had the nerve to suggest that I needed fixing, too. He said I believed lies as much as John did.

Excuse me?

John and I both remember clearly the scene in the elevator after we left Doug's office.

We stood in silence for a moment and then I said, "Well, he isn't God."

John laughed.

Mabel Collins famously said, "When the student is ready, the teacher will appear."[12] In our case, the teacher appeared, but we weren't ready.

Two years later we would be.

John:

Relief flooded me when Robbie made that remark after our session with Doug. I knew that pornography was wrong but I just didn't care. It was my "safe place". Any time I felt lonely, angry, tired or anything that wasn't comfortable, I would turn to fantasy, pornography and masturbation. My dilemma was that I loved my wife and wanted to please her, but I didn't trust her or anyone with my pain. All I could trust was my secret sex life.

When I was caught, I ran to shame and that shame was the thing that drove me to use again to avoid that bad feeling. Using was the opposite of what I had just promised, so of course it would lead to being caught again. Rinse and Repeat, Rinse and Repeat.

Robbie:

For the first seven years of our marriage we presented to the world a happy, fun-loving couple who led Bible Studies and loved Jesus. Inside our home, it was often a different picture. The denial that anything was wrong with our marriage covered the carpet, walls, and furniture like a fine layer of dust, dulling the shine of love.

God was about to blow His Spirit through our home removing all the dirt and leaving obvious open wounds and simmering lies we would have to deal with head on.

Section Two:

CAUGHT IN THE ACT

"…and you may be sure that your sin will find you out"
(Numbers 32:23).

Chapter Five

The Monster in the Corner

Pornography is a parasite, *because it steals your emotions, your focus, your time, your energy away from your spouse. I mean, it's really demonic, if you want to get down to it. Pornography is trying to meet a legitimate need in an illegitimate way. When you go down that path, you are not fulfilling each other as God intends for husband and wife and vice-versa, and it starts to degrade your marriage.*
—**Alex Kendrick**, *co-writer of movie, Fireproof*[13]

Robbie:

On a Wednesday night in February, John was at computer night school when I needed to check my email. We lived in a tiny cottage with a little room attached that we made into the office.

29

Our boy Noah was four years old at the time. I took him outside, and he played with his Stuart Little remote control car on the basketball court, as I sat in the office, door open, checking email. It wouldn't work. I kept clicking on my email link and nothing happened. I thought it might be frozen. I am not a computer gal, so I decided to get on John's email and see if I could retrieve my email through his account. It sounded logical at the time.

When I logged onto John's email, I clicked on history, thinking I would see my email address and get on that way. What I saw were a couple of shocking addresses.

"Noah."

"Yes, Mommy."

"I want you to see if you can make Stuart go around in circles for 10 whole seconds. Count out loud for me, okay?"

Eager for a game my boy said, "Okay," and the game was on.

"One!"

I prayed. "Lord, guide me. Guide me."

"Two!"

I clicked on the first address.

It was a picture God never intended to be taken.

"Three!"

I clicked back.

"Four!"

I clicked on the second website.

My heart pounded.

"Five!"

Tears welled up.

"Six!"

I clicked back.

"Seven!"

I turned off the computer.

"Eight!"

I prayed again. "What do I do, God? What do I do?"

"Nine!"

The Spirit was heavy on me. I felt completely calm. Shaming John into change never worked. For some reason, and I don't know exactly why, I made the decision to leave John. This thought had crossed my mind many times when we were arguing about pornography, but I never acted on it. He promised he would change and I believed him, even when it happened again and again. And I was too scared to leave. Fear of losing my marriage and fear of our family and our church friends finding out that we were not perfect stood in my way.

But on this night, my desperation trumped my fear. I could not and I would not raise Noah in a house where pornography lived. My reason to leave was not about me or my worth. I would develop that later. I left because I knew I had to protect Noah.

God impressed upon me that I should call my friend Theresa.

"Ten!"

"I did it, Mommy."

"Very good, Noah, keep playing. I am going to make a call."

Theresa and Jeff hosted the Bible Study we led and were faithful friends to John for years, even after his first marriage ended. I called Theresa and asked for prayer. I knew she would go to her knees immediately. Next I called Joani, my good friend who'd become an honorary Gamma for Noah. Then, I called my buddy Desha.

"Noah, let's go inside."

"Already?"

"It's getting dark, sweetie. But I have a surprise."

As I packed our bags, I told Noah he was going to get to visit Gamma and have a sleepover at her house. Noah was thrilled and started collecting toys to take.

I sat on our couch with a piece of paper and pen. I needed to leave John a note. The Spirit was with me and gave me peace. With no anger, I wrote a matter-of-fact letter to my husband.

In the car, for some reason I started thinking about *It's a Wonderful Life* and the scene where Mary Bailey tells her kids that their Dad, George, is in trouble.

"Should we pray?" Janie, the oldest girl, asked.

"Yes, pray hard." Mary answered.[14]

"Noah, let's pray for Daddy."

"Is he sick?"

"No, but he needs God's help, honey."

Noah's prayer was simple. "God, please help Daddy."

Just as the stars danced in the movie *It's a Wonderful Life* and God summoned Clarence the angel to go help George Bailey, I knew that my Lord in heaven blew the trumpet for help for John and our marriage.

Joani and Mark are dear friends of ours who have helped care for Noah since he was born. I taught their son in ninth grade and when he got married, Noah was the ring bearer. They are like family to me. Joani didn't ask questions. She just hugged me and told me she loved me.

I left and drove to my friend's condo.

I didn't want Noah to be around his crying Mommy. Desha, a faithful friend and fellow drama teacher, didn't ask questions either. Just showed me where I could sleep. Her mom was visiting and I sat with the two of them watching *West Wing* for a while. I was completely numb.

I knew I needed help. So I excused myself, got my Bible and went into Desha's bathroom. Lying down prostrate seemed the perfect thing to do. Desha happens to be a neat freak, so her floor was spotless. So in Desha's bathroom, I lay down and fell apart.

My tears came and relieved some of the immediate pain, like a good cry helps with a cut or bruise. In the midst of my wailing, I implored the King of all situations, "What do I do, God?" I'd recently heard a sermon about how we easily forget the truth God wants us to embrace daily. So I also prayed, "God, show me what You want me to remember."

I took my Bible and let it open where it might. I don't usually practice this, and I don't believe the open-your-Bible-and-point-at-a-verse method works ordinarily, but I was desperate. And I know that God shows up in special ways in desperate moments. He just does.

My Bible opened to Psalm 84. My eyes fell on this passage:

"Blessed are those whose strength is in you, whose hearts are set on pilgrimage. As they pass through the Valley of Baka, they make it a place of springs; the autumn rains also cover it with pools. They go from strength to strength, til each appears before God in Zion" (Psalm 84:5-7).

I took some deep breaths and let David's words sink in. *Set their hearts on pilgrimage. Set their hearts on pilgrimage.*

Perseverance is not my strong suit. I get bored easily. So easily that completion is something I have to pray for daily. I have several unfinished projects at all times. But this verse called me to keep going; it was a call for me to commit, to set my heart on the journey. Not necessarily the end line or the finished project. But I was to set my entire heart on the pilgrimage.

It would take heaven and earth to get me to quit the pilgrimage of mothering. The journey is tough at times, but my heart is committed. Likewise, writing is a pilgrimage full of rejection and joy and loneliness. But I have set my heart on it.

In that bathroom, God called me to keep going. To set my heart on the pilgrimage that is marriage.

At first I refused. "No!" I cried like a three-year-old girl who doesn't want to go to bed.

I loved Jesus. I had trusted Him to provide me with a Godly husband. But He had led me to a man who watched pornography all the time. My heart ached.

Yet, His Words of comfort kept coming to mind. In my mind's eye, He walked me through a lovely garden that evening and He promised a blessing. His Word didn't promise constant joy and it didn't promise reconciliation. In that garden, there was no guarantee that I wasn't going to get divorced. But there was a sweet, quiet assurance that God would be with me and that I would be blessed. I would walk through the Valley of Baka, (which is a dismal desert) but springs would come with autumn rains, providing moments of refreshment.

In the note I left for John, I didn't say I wanted a divorce. John and I had entered into marriage with a commitment to stay the course. I didn't want divorce. I wanted change.

I wanted the silent, deadly and horrid monster of pornography out of my house. It lived in a cob-webbed corner, hidden, but its tentacles touched everything. I'd known of its presence, but I didn't know how to fight it. Now it seemed like the Blob or one of those other creepy monsters from the 50s movies that grow uncontrollably.

"God, I can't do this."

Maybe divorce would be better. But how could I do that to Noah?

God's Holy Spirit reached down and gave me hope. Not answers, but hope. God's presence surrounded me.

Set your heart on the pilgrimage.

"Okay, Lord."

The pilgrimage would begin with suffering.

John:

I suffered every single day, but I had no idea of the pain to come. February 26, 2003 started out like any other day. I knew no reason it would end any differently than most. Like every weekday morning, our family got up and prepared for the day ahead. Shower, breakfast, get ready, and go. Routine. Robbie took Noah to preschool and went to her high school to teach. I hopped in my car to go to the community college where I taught computer classes before finishing up my homework for the night classes I attended.

Routine.

Teaching went well that day. It was a small school, and my classes consisted of a few adults wanting to find a job. I taught well and showed them how to dress for interviews. Many in my classes were ESL students, so I helped them read articles and further their understanding of English. I was a popular teacher because I gave so many smoke breaks. Little did they know I just wanted to act out.

My routine that day, like every day, included acting out. When I entered our marriage, I hoped that Robbie would deliver the happiness that I badly wanted. She didn't. The marriage didn't fill that hole in my soul either. The only thing that came close to giving me satisfaction in life was pornography and masturbation. On an average day, I would act out nine times. Like a junkie, I went through my days completely checked out and stoned.

Later, as I ate dinner and drove to the night school I attended, the same thoughts hounded me. *This is my life? There is nothing more?*

It was a combination of being a stoned zombie and a closet rageaholic. I was resentment looking for a place to happen. I was boiling underneath the surface, but sleepwalking through life.

Henry David Thoreau in his book *Walden* wrote,

The mass of men lead lives of quiet desperation. What is called resignation is confirmed desperation. From the desperate city you go into the desperate country, and have to console yourself with the bravery of minks and muskrats. A stereotyped but unconscious despair is concealed even under what are called the games and amusements of mankind.[15]

I was the epitome of one of those men. Quiet, desperate, living with unconscious despair.

When class ended, I headed home. As I parked, I saw that Robbie's car was gone.

Weird.

Lights were off in the house. It was empty.

She never goes out at night with Noah without telling me. Weird.

In the living room, I turned a light on and noticed a piece of paper on my recliner. I picked it up and read:

Dear John,

I found pornography on the computer. I can't do this anymore. I am not asking for a divorce. I am not. But I can't live in a house with pornography. Not with Noah here. I will call you.

Robbie

My heart dropped.

My wife had left me.

Not again. Dear God, not again.

I fell into my recliner, the world spinning. My first marriage ended because of my sexual acting out. I lost my wife and my daughters. I lost my job. Now my second marriage was a failure, too.

It was all happening again.

I sunk into a pit of despair. I had no idea where she was or how long she would stay away. For a long time, I didn't move. My old friend Shame sat with me. But then something occurred to me. *Wait. Robbie didn't ask for a divorce.* I read the note again. *She isn't going to divorce me. I won't lose everything again.*

The world stopped spinning, and my breathing returned to normal. I wasn't sure what was next. It would be painful, but she wasn't going to divorce me. Hope stirred.

If I am nice, say "Yes, dear," and apologize she will take me back. She's always forgiven me in the past. I will get through this.

It might be difficult for a while. I knew Robbie would be angry and pout and give me the silent treatment. But she would take me back. I wasn't ready to be a twice-divorced man. The shock dissipated, and I decided I would do what it took for her to come back.

Well, I will do whatever I need to for a while. I'm good at pretending.
She'll get over it.
But would she?

Chapter Six

The List

(And We're Not Talking Groceries)

Beginnings are always messy.
—John Galsworthy[16]

Robbie:

The first time I watched Richard Gere march into that paper factory and literally sweep Debra Winger off her feet in *An Officer and a Gentleman*[17] I laughed and cried. She took off his officer's hat, put it on her head, wrapped her arms around his neck and gave him a smile of victory. The swell of that song "Up Where We Belong"[18] and the cheers from her fellow workers made the scene one of those wonderful, memorable movie moments. I left the theatre smiling, a bit giddy. At the time I wasn't married, but I thought, yep, it is possible to have that kind of moment with my future husband.

When I woke up at Desha's house I stumbled back to the bathroom and saw the tile marks on my face like I was branded with lines of shame. I'd gotten a couple of hours of sleep in a bed, but the hours on the bathroom floor stared at me in the mirror. Felt right. No swell of music greeted me. Gone were the feelings of joy about the future of our relationship. I couldn't fathom feeling giddy about John ever again. The sweetness of happily-ever-after movie endings was about as far away from my heart as the notion to buy my beloved a Hallmark card.

Instead, I was hurt. And angry. And exhausted.

I was tempted to call in sick, but I didn't want to spend the day thinking and feeling. Better to work and concentrate on my students. I prayed God would help me, although I found my anger at Him was growing. He'd instructed me to set my heart on the pilgrimage of marriage. That resolve was going to be difficult to hang on to. Divorce would be easier. At the time I thought it would. I couldn't believe that God would allow this to happen to *me*.

After I picked up Noah from Gamma's and dropped him off at preschool, I went to work. I didn't have to teach until second period, so I decided to do some grading in the high school office.

My vice principal Laura read my face (she's very good at this) and called me into her office. "What's wrong with you?"

I sat in the chair across from her desk. "John..." Humiliation filled up my chest. "...is addicted to pornography." The last word came out like the forced confession of a criminal. It was out. Let the shaming begin.

Laura looked at me and said, "Robbie, it's just sin."

I will never forget that. Didn't she know that this was the ultimate sin? He was a sex addict, probably some kind of pervert and I, yes I Robbie Iobst, great Christian and great Christian teacher was married to him. Her words comforted me and simultaneously shocked me.

She must not know how horrible John's behavior was—this was not gossiping or lying or stealing. This was worse than any of those. God would bring to mind those four words, "Robbie, it's just sin," many times in the coming months.

As I left Laura's office, Cindy, the office manager noticed my mood and easily coerced me to spill the beans. After my rant of mortification, she asked, "Robbie, do you know any counselors?"

I thought about that moment in the elevator when I remarked that Doug wasn't God.

"Yes."

"Call him right now and get an appointment."

Doug just happened to have a cancellation that day after school. Yeah, right. There was no "just happened" about it. God knew. Doug welcomed me with compassion and grace. He listened as I bawled and let the confusion and anger I felt fall to the floor of his tidy therapist's office. "I need tangible help, Doug. Please tell me what to do."

"Let's pray first." Doug often stopped to pray. I loved that about him. We talked for a while, and he guided me to make a list of six requirements John needed to fulfill before I went back.

Then Doug added, "And Robbie, I would like you to join a group for wives of Christian sex addicts. A woman I work with leads it."

Vines of defensiveness sprouted up and coiled around my heart. John was the one with the problem, not me. "Why?"

Doug looked at me with a mix of compassion, professionalism, and brotherly love. "Because you married him, Robbie. You have some stuff to deal with, too."

You're not God.

My pride and desperation fought it out for a moment. Desperation for a marriage that worked won the battle. "When do I start?"

John:

After a couple of days, I finally got a call from Robbie. We awkwardly decided to meet at a Denny's and talk. On the drive to that restaurant, I felt a mix of emotions. Hope for the future, shame at my addiction, bravery because I managed a couple days of not acting out and, of course, cynicism. Robbie wasn't serious about all of this. She couldn't be. She'd take me back.

I arrived early and sat in a booth waiting for her. She was right on time, but it felt like I'd been waiting for hours. We exchanged hellos and I offered her a menu.

"I am not going to eat."

I noticed her eyes were puffy. "I'm sorry, Robbie." Maybe that would be the beginning of her coming home.

It wasn't. She told me she'd seen Doug.

"This time you have to change, John, or Noah and I are not going to live with you. Period."

Her voice showed no emotion. I didn't like this.

"And you need to do these six things."

She handed me a piece of paper. I couldn't help but think of the last piece of paper she'd given me. I sighed and realized that maybe this was not going to be as easy as I thought. I silently read the list. As I was perusing it, Robbie suddenly stood up. "Let me know what you are willing to do." With that, she left.

The list:

1. Tell our pastors.

I guess this was to be expected, and I assumed it was to humble me although it was going to feel more like humiliation. Robbie had often accused me of being a prideful man. I never understood what she was seeing. I was consumed with shame, and as such thought the worst about myself. I always assumed that pride meant thinking that I was better than everyone, not worse.

But I could do this one. I could tell our pastors. It would just be a lot more shame added to my plate. Robbie wanted to get back at me and this was a good start.

2. Quit leading Bible study.

This hurt. I needed to have an identity in our group of friends and fellow church goers. As a former pastor, being the one who knew more about the Bible than anyone else was the perfect identity for me. Leading Bible study was a cake walk. All I had to do was talk about what the verse or word meant. I never had to share my doubts, hurts, or feelings. Leading was a way to hide. I conceded to this because I felt it was temporary. I'd be back as the smartest person in the room soon enough.

3. Have our friend Jeff go through our computer files and clean out everything.

No problem here because I could always get more porn. However, it was embarrassing that she insisted it be Jeff. He'd known me years before when I was a pastor and when my first marriage failed. He knew why it had failed too. To have him know the details of why Robbie and I were having problems was humiliating.

4. Cancel internet access from our house.

Again, I felt this was not too difficult. At least there would be less temptation and again, if I wanted porn I could find it in places besides our home computer.

5. Commit to join Doug's group therapy of recovering Christian sex addicts.

I didn't even know what this meant. I had never been to group therapy, so I had no idea what to expect. I was embarrassed it was Doug leading. We had seen him before and I'd put on my best "everything is fine but Robbie is overacting" face. He was a consistent attendee at the church's men's ministry where I was a regular teacher, and now he was going to know I had been faking it.

6. Go back to a twelve step group for sex addiction.

I was most upset to see this on the list. I had gone to that fellowship before and was upset that they defined sex addiction as a spiritual problem with a spiritual solution. I was, after all, a pastor and clearly knew more about God than any of them. It never dawned on me to ask myself if I had the God thing all worked out, why was I powerless over lust, sex and porn? Years before, I had attended this fellowship for eighteen months while staying sober. I left because it wasn't Christian enough. Afterwards, I almost immediately went back to acting out. I couldn't admit that they were right, so I stayed away for eight and a half years. Now I was on the brink of destroying another marriage.

I took the list home and read it over and over. I made the decision and began the process of completing each item. Then I called Robbie. A few days after she left me, she moved back home.

We lived under the same roof, but we had never been farther apart. She made it clear that moving back in with me did not equal forgiveness. We didn't laugh about the whole thing, like I thought we might. We didn't laugh about anything.

I would soon find out that Robbie wasn't "getting over" the hurt and expected me to follow through with my commitment to the list.

Chapter Seven

The First Two Lessons

(or We Are Worth the Work)

A little boy was having difficulty lifting a heavy stone. His father came along just then. Noting the boy's failure, he asked, "Are you using all your strength?"

"Yes, I am," the little boy said impatiently.

"No, you are not," the father answered. "I am right here just waiting, and you haven't asked me to help you.

—Anonymous[19]

Robbie:

"I want you to make a list of five things you do just for yourself." Betty, my counselor, assigned me this after our first session together.

"Why do I have to make a list?" My eyes burned from crying. "I shouldn't have to do anything. This is John's problem, and John is the one who needs to make lists, not me."

Betty was a Godly Christian counselor who had a heart for hurting women. Her practice was in the same building as Doug's, and she led a group for women married to or dating Christian sex addicts.

Our first two appointments were one-on-one, and then I would join the group. As we sat together, I couldn't deny the fact that she resembled my mother in many ways. Tall, slim, immaculately groomed with an air of reservation about her. And her smile was beautiful just like my own mom's. However, the similarities ended there. My mother would roll over in her grave if she knew that I was about to talk about my private problems to someone who was not family. That would be bad enough, but to actually pay good hard-earned money to that person to listen? Sally Floyd would not understand or approve. I didn't plan on telling my father, either, although I sensed he would be more open. He'd say, "Rob, it's your life."

At the end of our first session I began to think maybe Mama's views were right. I didn't need to be here. Tears bubbled out with pain and I blubbered. "Why do I need to show you a list of my hobbies, Betty? Are we going to cross-stitch, or are we going to talk about John's problem?"

She responded in that annoying and gentle therapist way that both angered me and comforted me. "Robbie you married him. You chose him. So we have to look at what is going on in your heart."

Her words were very close to what Doug told me. I scoffed and told Betty I'd do it. That night I thought I should do it quickly and get it over with. But when I sat down with pen and paper, something weird happened. I couldn't think of anything I did just for me. Before I married, I used to do all sorts of activities. I loved to write and read. I didn't write often anymore. I enjoyed going to the theatre, I played the piano and I loved swimming. But none of these had been penciled in my calendar for a long time.

So instead of scribbling down a list of my hobbies, I made a mental note.

I am too busy for silly activities. I teach. I serve at the church a lot. I take care of Noah and John. When you're married and a mom, you have different priorities.

At the next session I was cocked and ready to shoot my reasons and defend myself. Why did she ask me to do this anyway?

Betty countered my defensiveness with some wisdom I didn't want to hear. The list I couldn't write revealed more about me than a so-called busy schedule. Throughout our seven years of marriage, I had buried parts of myself. The things that make me Robbie. The joys I got from life. It wasn't that I didn't go to the theatre or play the guitar anymore. That wasn't the point. The point was that I stopped doing those things because I felt I needed to spend that time with John, for John, to be loved by John.

As I discovered his weaknesses, I started a little program to change him. It became very important to me to make him look good, no matter what. I became his PR rep at church. More of him and less of me. In doing this, I was clinging to the illusion that he was the Godly man I dreamed of marrying. The Godly man that loved me completely. Now it was my job to make sure he became that Godly man. With all this work to do on John, how could I find time to write or go swimming?

Lesson number one: It was time to make caring for my heart the priority in my life. I was worth it.

I began living this verse: "Above all else, guard your heart, for everything you do flows from it" (Proverbs 4:23). I'd neglected my heart and my true identity for too long.

In order to heal this part of me and bring back my individuality to our marriage, I began the process of what I called "un-velcroing" myself from John. It was no longer my job to make him look good. He was his own person and so was I. Instead of using all that time to prove to everyone what a great man he was, I now used it to take care of my own issues. I began the process of discovering that I was lovable and loved. As I did this, I began listening to God more.

But it was just the beginning of a difficult year of working to save our marriage. The day I attended the group for wives of Christian sex addicts for the first time was a horrible day. I arrived late at my job, I felt sick and nauseous and somehow, despite the first days of "un-velcroing," I decided that everything that went wrong in our marriage was probably my fault.

I'd left John three weeks earlier. After I'd handed him the list Doug gave me, he went right to work on it, completing it quickly. Noah and I moved back in after a few days. Now we lived together but rarely spoke. During our silence, I solved the entire problem. John must be a sex addict because I couldn't satisfy him sexually. Maybe I wasn't adventurous enough. I was a fat woman who didn't deserve love, and therefore robbed her husband of a gratifying relationship. It was all me.

I didn't want to go to Betty's and admit all of this. On the other hand, I knew that when I walked into her group I would see five other ugly, fat women like me. Maybe it would be good to share our shame.

Over cupcakes, perhaps.

I'd set my heart on pilgrimage, so I went ahead to the group meeting. My heart was petrified and angry and defensive and so very sad.

When I opened the door to Betty's office, I looked around at the smiling faces greeting me. And their bodies. To my amazement, I sat in a room with five beautiful women. I would learn that one was a physical trainer and one was a former model. All five were physically fit with no horrible scars or deformities.

My second lesson: John's addiction was his thing, his problem. Not mine. It had nothing to do with me or the size of my bottom or the prowess I possessed in the bedroom.

I would become very familiar with the three C's.

I did not CAUSE his addiction.

I could not CURE his addiction.

I could not CONTROL his addiction.

I cried as I drove home from that first group meeting. But this time the tears were not shameful or sad. I cried in thanksgiving. In Betty and those five women, God had given me six gifts. Six women who would understand, walk with me, and teach me how to survive the journey. Truth started inching in.

During the next weeks and months, the time I spent with Betty and the gals would be some of the most eye-opening of my life. My heart, in painful labor, gave birth to epiphanies and lessons each week.

John:

I had one-on-one meetings with Doug several times. Then we scheduled a session with Robbie, too. That hour was vastly different than our time with Doug a couple of years previously. Robbie's anger and my shame were in full view, not masked with denial. At the end of my time with Doug and Robbie, I learned I was sufficiently contrite enough to be invited into group therapy with other sex addicts.

Oh boy.

I hated every second, but I knew that Robbie would get over it eventually. So I decided to go for a while.

The group had some entrance requirements:

1. Must be a Christian.

2. Must be a Sex Addict

3. Must be invited into the group by Doug.

To graduate the group, each member needed to complete all twelve steps from a workbook along with a relapse prevention plan. It would take about a year or so to complete all of the assignments, and only when a member graduated did a seat come open. I am not sure what Doug saw in me during those few meetings, but I was placed on the top of the waiting list and invited to my first session a few weeks later. During that time, I returned to a twelve step fellowship and remained sober. The term "sober" meant having no sex with myself or with anyone to whom I wasn't married. Given the hurt and broken trust I caused Robbie, we weren't having sex either so I was completely celibate and miserable.

The first night in the group I was asked to tell my story. I knew this was all temporary so I held nothing back. Why not? I told them about my first exposure to pornography at age eight, my being molested at age eleven, and how my addiction ended my first marriage and drove me out of the pastorate. I ended my tale by telling the men about my current obsession with pornography and masturbation that was about to end my second marriage.

Lesson one: I was not the only one. I knew that I was not the only sex addict in the world, but that day I discovered I was not the only Christian sex addict. In fact, I was to learn that the church is full of sex addicts, especially in this age of the internet, which is the opium of sex addiction. Doug turned out to be a good counselor who possessed a real anointing for helping Christian men untangle the knots of guilt, shame and sexuality while all the time pointing us back to Jesus.

In one of those first few sessions, I broke down and admitted that I just didn't have any faith that I could really change. I had after all, been to a twelve step fellowship for sex addiction and counseling before and it didn't provide any lasting change. I had tried to stop many, many times and it had never worked. Why should I believe that this time would be any different? Although I confessed this to them, secretly my only hope was that maybe Robbie would "get over it" and we could get back to pretending. But I didn't know if I could last that long. I was ready to give up.

I'll never forget the group's response. They assured me it was okay that I didn't believe, and it was fine that I felt the process would not work for me. Instead of worrying about my lack of faith in the process, they asked me to use their faith and lean on them. They would believe *for* me. They told me to lean on them until my faith grew.

I sat stunned, staring at these men.

Until then, my life had been filled with secrecy and lying. I knew if other men knew the truth about me, they would know I didn't have what it took to be a real man and they would reject me. This group of men, this band of brothers, saw the real me and accepted me. Just as I was. They believed in me and encouraged me.

Lesson number two: if I didn't have enough faith to believe I could get through this, I just needed to borrow someone else's faith.

Doug and the others reminded me of the friends of the paralyzed man in the Bible in the Gospel of Mark.

"A few days later, when Jesus again entered Capernaum, the people heard that he had come home. They gathered in such large numbers that there was no room left, not even outside the door, and he preached the word to them. Some men came, bringing to him a paralyzed man, carried by four of them. Since they could not get him to Jesus because of the crowd, they made an opening in the roof above Jesus by digging through it and then lowered the mat the man was lying on. When Jesus saw their faith, he said to the paralyzed man, 'Son, your sins are forgiven'" (Mark 2:1-5).

The man's friends carried him to Jesus for healing, but they couldn't get to Jesus. They didn't give up or leave. Instead, they went the extra mile to carry their friend to healing.

I was paralyzed in my addiction and could not do anything for myself. Doug and the men in that group picked me up and carried me to Jesus. They knew the way to Jesus when I didn't. They brought me to Him even though I assumed He would reject me. Verse 5 says "When Jesus saw *their* faith..." The men in Doug's group brought me to Jesus because they had faith when I didn't.

Robbie's first two lessons apply to anyone in a relationship with an addict.

1. **Your life and heart are important. Care for them because you are worth it.**
2. **Your spouse's addiction has nothing to do with you. You didn't cause it, you can't cure it, and you can't control it.**

My first two lessons apply to any addict.

1. **You are not the only one. You are not alone.**
2. **If you don't have the faith to believe you can recover, someone else does. Borrow their faith.**

As difficult as this process began, we both started inching our way to recovery. But was reconciliation possible? We both had many lessons to go.

Chapter Eight

Visions Through Dreams

"I will praise the Lord, who counsels me
even at night my heart instructs me"
(Psalm 16:7).

Robbie:

Anger became a roommate for us, sitting at meals, lying in the middle of our bed, casting a spell over long commutes in the car. Therapy was teaching me and changing me. I was discovering how addiction affected marriage and how I had been an enabler. I found strength in me that I didn't know was there. Strength that would lead to the ability to change myself and how I acted and reacted.

Although I was learning, I was still furious at John.

And I was furious with God.

The unfairness of my situation hit me and I yelled at Him more than once.

"God, I have never turned from you. I haven't. I said yes to You when I stood below that West Texas sky when I was eight years old. I was a Jesus girl growing up. I hardly ever missed church, I was active in the youth group and I was a summer missionary—I have been employed in Christian ministries, I have led people to Jesus, and I teach at a Christian school. Come on! All I have ever asked for is a Godly husband. This has been my heart's desire. And what do You, the God of all, give me? A sex addict? Come on!"

In my tirades, I heard nothing from God. No direction, no promises and no apology. But the God of the Universe finally answered. He did it through a dream.

John and I officially stopped leading our Bible study after I left him, but we still visited. Jeff and Theresa, the hosts of the study, had stepped in to lead. Jeff asked us to come so they could pray us through the journey of counseling and reconciliation.

In their living room, we joined in worship and Bible study. We didn't comment much, but were always greeted and loved on by our friends. We were open wounds, bleeding badly. Our home group nursed us gently.

During one of those nights, John made a comment on the study. Normally, this would have been no big deal. But whatever he said struck a match of anger in me and I began to burn. I sat glaring at him, wondering how in the world he could call himself a Christian. How in the world did he think he deserved to offer an opinion on anything spiritual? Tears stung my eyes with fury. I was done. I was finished with the therapy and the whole shebang.

We drove home in silence, except for sweet Noah talking about playing with the other kids at Bible Study. When we arrived back at our place, Noah went to bed and then me. Not even a goodnight to my husband.

Most nights I dream silly, wild dreams that make no sense or ones I don't remember. But that night God gave me a dream I would never forget.

I was swimming in a big beautiful pool of clear blue water. The sun shone and its warm rays shimmered on the water. The heat radiated off the cement. An azure sky held no clouds, just a beautiful backdrop to joy. This was my favorite season, my favorite feeling. Swimming in a pool on a summer day. I felt happy and content.

Suddenly, everything changed. The pool became black tar and I couldn't swim. I felt stuck, and the rubbery, sticky tar made my skin crawl. The stench nauseated me while my stomach felt as if it was running laps inside me.

A deep voice that I knew belonged to God said to me, "Robbie do you know what this is?"

Of course I did. "Yes, God. This tar is John's sin and I am stuck in the middle of it."

"No, Robbie. This is your sin. Only yours. But I can help you out of it."

I saw a hand at the side of the pool.

"Let me help you."

I woke up sweating.

It took a while for me to realize that maybe I was not just some innocent victim brutalized by her husband's addiction. Maybe, just maybe, I was part of the problem in our marriage. At first, I found this difficult to swallow, but the dream God gave me made it clear. I didn't bring sex addiction to our union, but I brought an insecurity and obsession with my weight. I also brought a startling amount of self-righteousness.

Doug and Betty's words started making sense. Betty explained to me that when someone chooses their mate, they often choose their psychological equal. In this case, I chose John because he was what I deserved. I didn't want to know about the addiction even when John brought it to my attention, but there were red flags during our dating that made me wonder about his level of spirituality. And yet, I didn't question anything, because I was desperate to be loved. Yes, I definitely had "stuff" in me that wasn't God's best. I realized that the swimming pool of black tar needed to be dealt with in order to save our marriage. This changed everything for me.

John:

When I go to sleep, I'm out; I just disappear. It's how God made me. It can be frustrating to Robbie because she never sleeps long or well, and she has watched me sleep and commented later that I looked like a corpse – immovable, barely breathing. As if I were a newborn baby, Robbie has poked me several times, just to make sure I was breathing, or so I've been told.

So I don't have dreams, at least none that I ever remember. But around the same time God gave Robbie that dream, He gave me one, too. He definitely works in mysterious ways.

In my dream, I walked into a large room, spacious and a bit dark but the kind of room that is useful for tasks besides sleeping or storage. The floor was carpet, utilitarian and inexpensive, and when I looked closely, I saw stains throughout. No furniture. Just emptiness. Space. I walked to the center of the room and it occurred to me that this would be the last time the room would appear this way. I wasn't sure why. When my eyes began to look over the walls recognition came.

This was an art gallery.

Even though I am not a fan of art, the feeling struck me as comfortable, like when I put my sweats on at the end of the day. But the pictures weren't old. Or were they?

I walked closer to the first one. It was a painting. I glanced around and noticed all the framed art was oil painted or photographed. The walls were filled.

Each had words written across the bottom.

I began to read. My lungs constricted and I gasped for air. The words on the first painting, blurred until now, came into focus. It was a curse from a teacher, "You will never be anything…"

The next one came from a relative. I couldn't make out what the painting was, but the words were clear. My heart began to hurt.

I stood in a gallery of wounds.

I spied a mantle in the middle of the room with lights above it illuminating one particular picture. It depicted me and my father on the phone to each other. My familiar father wound, "So you're going to be a preacher? You'll be good at that. All the men in our family have been con men."

Not all the wounds were caused by others. Some were consequences of my own sins. Standing in the midst of all that pain was too much to bear.

I sensed the door behind me opened, ushering in the presence of God.

Why was I here and why was God here? Ashamed, I couldn't turn around to look at Him. Was I dead? Was this judgment? I stood frozen.

A man in white painters' clothes appeared beside me with a bucket of paint, a brush and a roller. He said nothing but I knew it was Jesus. He took the biggest artwork down. The painting of my father wounding me was gone and a faded square was left on the wall.

Jesus handed me a roller. "Help me put a new coat of paint on the wall."

I took it and began. I didn't understand how new paint would matter when the same shameful art was hung again, but I pushed the roller up and down until the job was done. Jesus bent down and picked up the artwork and hung it on the newly painted wall. Much to my surprise, the picture had changed. The centerpiece to the exhibit was a painting of me at peace, standing in a beautiful valley. The words etched below said "Beloved Son of a Loving Father and King."

In that moment, I realized shame defined my identity. Sometimes that voice belonged to my father or my teachers but the message was always shame. All that time God, too, spoke to me about my identity but I couldn't or wouldn't hear Him because the voice of shame was louder. Shame convinced me God couldn't love someone like me.

I woke up.

As I continued the painful journey of recovery, I often pictured my gallery of wounds. I had hung countless paintings there. It was time to allow God to renovate that room in my heart. That dream did not magically heal my identity but it gave me a vision of what my recovery would resemble.

Our dreams redefined our reality. Robbie had believed she was a good Christian and a victim of my sin. I had believed I was just bad to my core and a victimizer.

Robbie:

Our dreams helped us turn a corner. John began a real relationship with the living God, the Father, not a deity that resembled his dad. I began to understand that I was not a victim, but a participant in this marriage. I was a part of the problem and I could be a part of the solution.

However, the next step to reconciliation scared me to death.

Chapter Nine

Furniture Moving Day

Confession is good for the soul.
—Scottish proverb [20]

Robbie:

"This is a healthy choice, Robbie." Betty's gray eyes pierced me. My fellow therapy-ladies looked at me with compassion, agreeing with Betty.

"But what if I don't want to know? What if he says something I don't want to hear?"

Betty nodded. "I understand. This is completely your decision, but if you want total honesty in your relationship, this is a good first step."

That night after Noah was asleep in his bed, I broached the subject with John. "I would like to know everything, John. Everything about your behavior as a sex addict."

"What? Are you sure?" He tilted his head in confusion.

"Yes. Full disclosure. I need to know it all."

John stared at the ground for a few minutes. In the silence, I wondered if I really did want to know all of it. Did I really want to know how many sex partners John had in the past? Did I really need to know when he had lied to me and how? I was asking for pain. I might as well have asked him to shoot me in the leg.

John sighed. I saw the reluctance in his eyes. He wasn't happy. "Okay." He got up to get ready for bed.

As I fell asleep, I said the words over and over: *Set my heart on the pilgrimage, set my heart on the pilgrimage.*

John:

I felt trapped by her request. My working philosophy of life was "If you knew the truth about me you would leave me." So I was caged in an impossible dilemma. If I refused to cooperate with Robbie, she would leave me, but if I told her everything, she would leave me.

I said yes, because it was the next step.

We decided not to have this discussion at home with Noah around, so we made an appointment to go to a bay in San Diego to sit and talk.

Robbie:

At school, I told Cindy about our plans.

"Sounds like you are going to move furniture." She remarked.

"What?"

"It's an old metaphor for confrontation. One person is carrying a chair, which represents a burden and they need to get rid of it. By telling the other person, the burden can be shared. When two people carry the chair, it is light and easy to set down."

So John and I began moving furniture. John brought sofas and recliners. I brought a china hutch. Rules were simple. I could ask him anything. He answered honestly.

Time and again, he shocked me with details of his dark, secret path. I was no saint, but sexual impurity had never been a challenge for me. It was too much for one day. Each time I hit overload we would leave. Three times we sat in our car looking out at the majestic Pacific Ocean. As I gazed out on all that blue beauty, I sat in the ugliness of John's past. We talked as we'd never talked before. I cried. I yelled. I found out everything.

John:

Robbie asked pointed questions. She wanted to know details about the frequency of my acting out and the types of pornography I used. She asked me about certain situations where she had sensed dishonesty. More than once, I confirmed her feelings. When we talked about all of those times she had found pornography and lectured me, I told her I knew I wouldn't stop, even as I said "never again."

It was like having dental surgery. Horrible and painful. I knew that in my full disclosure I was ending my marriage. One thing surprised me, though. Robbie insisted that my lying was the most hurtful act. More painful than the specific quantity of pornography, masturbation and the dark choices I'd made.

Robbie:

To me, those awful hours weren't dental surgery, but labor. Intense, painful labor. But as in labor, something wonderful was birthed. We began to shoulder each other's burdens in our marriage. John's past was his past, not mine, but as he opened up to me, I began to see him for who he was, not the fairy tale Godly preacher I wanted him to be. John took on my anger and carried the pain of betrayal with me in a way that only gut-wrenching honesty can facilitate. As we sat in our car, the ocean's rippling water brought in fresh life with each wave. A sense of newness.

After those three miserable, horrible, wonderful appointments, we'd emptied a moving truck of burdens and split the weight evenly between the two of us. Not all the furniture was put away. That would take years. But now we shared the load.

John:

We entered new territory. A marriage of complete honesty. Much to my surprise, the truth didn't destroy us. It broke up the hard ground of our hearts, so that God could plant new seeds. Now it was up to God to decide what seeds to plant.

Robbie:

One of those plants He nurtured in me tore my heart up, as its branches broke through the rigid dirt of control.

Chapter Ten

Get Out of my Way

God created man, but I could do better.
—Erma Bombeck[21]

Robbie:

"I like how you're changing." One of my fellow group therapy members, herself married to a sex addict, made this observation as we walked into the parking lot after a session.

"What do you mean by that?"

"You are talking more about yourself and less about your husband."

"So?"

"I think it's a powerful step when we stop saying 'my husband needs to be fixed' and start saying, 'I need to look at myself.'"

I wanted to say, "You're dead to me," and never talk to her again.

But I realized she was correct. Ever since my dream, I'd been thinking about that black tar and asking the Father how in the world I could break free.

During this season of recovery, a war broke out between John and me every Sunday morning. Church was at the center of the battle. I believed that attending church was one of the best ways for us to reconcile our marriage. The presence of God was there. Many of our friends would be there, too.

We needed to go to church.

We should go to church.

John better go to church.

His opinions varied about this. Some Sundays he wanted to go, but most times he wanted to stay home. On those particular mornings, I would put on my best passive-aggressive outfit, humph around the house while getting Noah and I ready and leave. Then I'd slam the door behind us. *There! He'll see.*

I didn't understand my husband. Apparently, I didn't know him either. I assumed he would instinctively know that God and church were the pathways to healing. He refused both.

He didn't read the Bible.

He didn't go to church.

He didn't pray with me except at night which was our habit and even then, he wasn't engaged.

He even refused to have a quiet time.

I'd married a sex addict heathen who was bent on never changing. Our marriage had no hope.

One Sunday morning, I asked him if he wanted to go to church with Noah and me and he said, "No." The way he said it communicated to me that he was tired of the question. Filled with fury, I banged doors so hard the hinges almost fell off.

In church during worship, I remembered the black tar. I thought about my heathen husband. He wasn't ever going to change. Anger and self-pity filled me up, even as I tried to sing the words praising Jesus.

Then, I heard God. Clear as a bell in my heart, He said, *Robbie, get out of My way.* Shocked, I sat down. *What God?*

Get out of My way.

He proceeded to tell me that I stood between He and John. Apparently, my attempts at trying to control John's spirituality and how he related to God was a huge pain to the Father and didn't help accomplish anything. God told me to get out of His way and let Him and John have their own relationship free of me, my nagging, my passive-aggressiveness and my self-righteousness.

How? I asked.

I never thought God would ever say the following words to me but He did. Again as clear as ever, in my heart I heard five words. *Shut up about anything spiritual.*

So I did. I resolved to not talk to John about God, church, prayer or the Bible. I gave myself a three-month deadline, so if it were too difficult I could remind myself it was just for a while.

The first time I held my tongue was akin to swimming against a strong current. It felt wrong. But I obeyed and as I did I heard, *Pray for him. Silently and a lot. Use My Word.*

I found a 3" by 5" notecard and looked through the Bible. I decided on Colossians 1:9-14. I wrote it on my notecard, personalizing the Scriptures for John.

"For this reason, since the day we heard about John, we have not stopped praying for John. We continually ask God to fill John with the knowledge of God's will through all the wisdom and understanding that the Spirit gives, so that John may live a life worthy of the Lord and please him in every way: bearing fruit in every good work, growing in the knowledge of God, being strengthened with all power according to

His glorious might so that John may have great endurance and patience, and giving joyful thanks to the Father, who has qualified John to share in the inheritance of His holy people in the kingdom of light. For God has rescued John from the dominion of darkness and brought John into the kingdom of the Son he loves, in whom we have redemption, the forgiveness of sins."

R.C. Sproul said "Prayer does change things, all kinds of things. But the most important thing it changes is us."[22]

And it did. As I clutched that notecard, the Spirit changed my heart toward my husband and toward God. I kept that card with me wherever I went and prayed those words over and over for three months. I clung to the hope God would do a work in me and in John. The Lord did not disappoint.

Over time, I recognized my pride for what it was, a wall that kept me from living in the fullness of God's presence. I saw my own struggle with food for what it was, a way to cope with pain instead of going to God. I began examining my wounds and tried to grow in the confidence that I was completely and fully loved. I admitted to myself that I had watched pornography before I met John. My holier-than-thou saintly Robbie act was a facade. As I prayed for my beloved, I realized that forgiveness was possible and vital to the rest of our marriage.

I asked God for forgiveness for thinking I knew better than Him. I needed to forgive myself for lying to myself and John. As I prayed for John, I naturally prayed for myself, to become the kind of woman, wife and mother God wanted me to be.

One night I asked John to meet me after work at a Mexican food place near my high school. After we were seated, he asked me what was up.

"I want to ask for your forgiveness." Just as he had given me the details of his sin when we were moving furniture, I shared the sin I harbored in my heart toward him. "Will you forgive me?"

John chuckled and said, "Of course. But will you forgive me?"

I'd never said the words. It was time to tell him. "I forgive you, John."

We left the restaurant and went home. The conversation didn't end in a hug or kiss. We continued our abstinence as we had for months. My hurt and anger didn't disappear that night. It was only a step in the journey, but a critical, vital step. God was at work in me and in John. As we allowed Him more space and voice in our marriage, change crept in.

One Sunday morning, near the end of my three months of silence John asked me in a cheerful voice, "Wanna go to church?"

It was good to get out of God's way.

Chapter Eleven

Of Course I Feel that Way

Addiction is a forgetting disease, but I forgot that.
—**Anonymous**[23]

John:

For the first ninety to one hundred days of sobriety, every day felt worse than the day before. It was as if someone had climbed into my head and turned the volume up all the way and then removed the knobs. Withdrawal. Acting out had become an integral part of every day of my life. So much so, that when I went cold turkey my body chemistry went crazy. Pain woke me up in the morning and put me to bed at night. Several times each day I thought about using porn and acting out. I knew I would experience temporary relief, but then I would have to experience all this again, or worse. Since I didn't know how long the pain would last, I played a trick on myself.

"What if tomorrow will be the day it gets better? It sure isn't today, but what if it's tomorrow?" And so I would get through the day sober.

Around day 100, I woke up and the noise in my head was quieter. The withdrawal symptoms began to lessen. In the absence of constant pain, I began to think more clearly. The fog lifted.

Eventually, I began to see that the real consequence of my addiction wasn't Robbie's disapproval. The real consequence was internal; I was separated from my heart and from God. I lived life in my head. I finally started to do the work of recovery for myself, not Robbie. It got a bit easier. But it also got more difficult because now I needed to actually change. The old saying goes, nothing changes if nothing changes, and if I keep doing what I've always done, I'll keep getting what I've always got, and will keep feeling what I always felt. —Anonymous [24]

Changing my internal thoughts and beliefs was as vital, if not more important, than changing my behavior - a deal breaker if I was to remain sober. I needed to deal with my father issues and the way they polluted my image of God. Recovery required me to change two things:

1. My image of God
2. Everything else

The changes needed to come in that order.

Life and recovery got easier because I could now stop becoming the man Robbie had dreamed of and instead, become the man I was. I just needed to feel the feelings and do the work.

I began with firing God. When I tell other believers I fired God, I usually get a look that says, "you blasphemer". How ridiculous to presume I have the power to fire the Creator of the Universe.

But my image of God contributed to my addiction, in that it provided shame which gave me pain so I acted out to get rid of the pain. When I considered God, I saw someone who looked a lot like my father. And that meant God didn't believe I was worth anything just like the man I'd met when I was 19. I could never get God's approval and I would always be "less than" in His eyes.

A day came when I fired that image of God. I prayed, "Okay, God, if You are really real, please teach me who You really are."

In my mind, lust was a dragon in my life, attacking me constantly. When I decided to get sober, I picked up my sword and began to fight back. In fact, over the years I tried to stop using pornography many times. But the dragon always won. During my first months of recovery, it occurred to me this new God of mine was standing behind me as I fought the dragon.

So I asked, 'God, are you going to help me or what?" I mean, why wasn't He defeating this dragon for me?

In my heart, God told me, *You think the fight is yours. You keep using your sword to fight. Maybe you need to put the sword down. It's not your fight anyway.*

I dropped the sword. But still the dragon was there. Constantly breathing his fiery breath of temptation on me.

"God, you still aren't fighting him. Do something."

You need to trust Me.

"What? I put the sword down."

But you are still facing the dragon.

If I turned around and faced God, I knew what would happen. All my life I believed if I met God face to face, the first thing He would do is roll His eyes. Disappointment would cover His face.

It was one of the most difficult decisions of my life, but I turned away from fighting lust, and faced God.

I was shocked. All I saw was beauty. And love, lots of love.

God showed me my fight against lust and sex addiction was only to be won through making the choice daily, sometimes moment by moment, to turn away from the fight and face God. It was His fight.

As I grew in recovery, I noticed the dragon did not leave. He never left. I asked God, "Why is lust still here? Why don't you destroy it once and for all?"

Because the dragon is the one thing in your life that brings you to your knees. The dragon can remind you the fight is mine. "The Lord will fight for you; you need only to be still" (Exodus 14:14).

One of the most memorable moments in the group counseling meetings was the night that one of the guys in my group shared a story about his recovery from alcohol. He was home alone one night, the family was away and he was making dinner. In the refrigerator was an open bottle of wine and he had the thought that he could have some and no one would ever know. Then he had the thought, *Of course I feel that way, I'm an alcoholic.*

That statement was such an epiphany to me; I could talk to myself about recovery and remind myself of my powerlessness. After some time sober, a thought creeps into most addicts' thinking that goes something like "Now that I have been sober for X number of days, weeks, months or years, I should be able to resist temptation."

In other words, most believe that after a certain amount of time the addict is no longer really powerless. This is a lie; powerless is powerless. In fact, this is a common belief about the twelve steps. In step one, I admit that I'm powerless; then in the remaining eleven steps I get my power back. The truth is that in the first step I admit my powerlessness and in the remaining eleven steps I learn to be at peace with that powerlessness.

The lie that I am no longer powerless carries a strong message of shame when I am tempted. The lie says I shouldn't feel or react that way when tempted or triggered. Simply saying, "Of course I feel that way, I'm a sexaholic," dismisses the shame and I am free to surrender my right to lust about that person, place or thing. From that day to now when I'm tempted or triggered, I say, out loud if possible, these three things:

1. Of course I feel that way, I'm a sexaholic.
2. I surrender my right to lust about _____. I fill in that blank with as much specific detail as possible.

3. I pray for that woman that God would bless and care for her and that He would protect her from being an object of lust to anyone. She is someone's daughter, wife, girlfriend or mom.

This is a form of surrender. Surrender is critical to recovery and staying sober, but it is very counterintuitive. Our internal beliefs tell us that to defeat any temptation, we must fight. The problem with that is it assumes that we have the power to win that fight. Powerlessness settles that argument. Since I'm powerless I can't win the fight, so the best thing I can do is not get pulled into the fight. Surrender is simply admitting this is not my fight to win, that God will fight for me, so I'll let Him.

"Of course I feel that way" is my decision to surrender who I am to God, who knows and loves me enough to fight for me.

"He rescued me from my powerful enemy, from my foes, who were too strong for me. They confronted me in the day of my disaster, but the LORD was my support" (Psalm 18:17-18). It is His fight.

Chapter Twelve

These Three Things

Life is a succession of lessons which must be lived to be understood.
—Helen Keller [25]

John:

Ever since the fall in Genesis 3, we humans have had a bent towards independence. Each of us is like a car with bad alignment that always pulls to the right and requires consistent left force on the steering wheel just to go down the road. It takes a lot of work and the tires are being ruined.

All of us have the same misalignment; we are all traveling in a similar circle. If we compare our lives with other people, we assume we are all going in the right direction. Addicts like me always try to deal with our pain and problems with a solution other than God. Since it (the object of our addiction) seems to work, we use again and again until it takes on a life of its own. Leaving us with not only a misalignment, but a compelling reason to isolate and hide from everyone including ourselves and God.

I discovered that I had tendencies towards a way of living that, while not specific to my acting out addiction, were unhealthy and were major supporters of the addiction. Each in its own way needed to be stopped and replaced with a new way of living. In the next few pages I will describe three of those unhealthy ways of living and the healthy alternative that I have learned and tried to incorporate into my daily living.

Time Travel vs. Being Present

Although I didn't own a time machine, my tendency was to spend most of my time thinking about my past or fantasizing about the future. In my case, it was often about reliving past sexual experiences and imagining future experiences I thought might meet some unmet need. When I took a trip to the past, I was overcome by shame for what I had done and regret for what I didn't do. When I journeyed to the future, I would quickly be overcome by fear of tragedy, failure and disappointment.

As I grew in recovery, I realized when I traveled to the past or future, God was never with me.

One of my friends in recovery asked me a strange question, "Who's sober tomorrow?"

I assumed he was encouraging me to try harder to be sure that I would be "sober tomorrow". But the correct answer was *no one*. All we have is today. When time traveling to the future, I can't be sober, and when I time traveled to the past I usually went to a time I was not sober. I could not stay sober if I didn't learn to live one day at a time and learn to be at peace no matter how uncomfortable.

We have all heard the saying, "No pain, no gain." I had my own saying, "No pain is just fine with me." My entire life was about avoiding discomfort, so I used my addiction to minimize it in my life. My pain avoidance became the avoidance of all feelings. Until I was willing to feel pain, I couldn't feel joy or love. The irony of addiction is that while I was looking for love and acceptance, the result was that I could experience neither because I refused to stay present to any feelings at all.

The solution is to stay present and learn to live one day at a time.

Time travel in our marriage was just another way I wasn't available to Robbie. I would never be present to feel what was going on; instead, I would go back in time to some perceived wrong that Robbie had done so I was "justified" in my resentments and acting out. Time travel hurt our marriage. Staying present to what my wife is experiencing in our marriage is vital to a healthy marriage.

So how do I make myself stay off the time travelling machine?

I make a conscious choice to slow down.

I practice breathing.

I intentionally choose to pay close attention to what is in front of me.

Being present is vital to recovery.

Isolation vs. Community

Men in general, and addicts in particular, tend to live isolated lives. God the Father, Son and Holy Spirit is, are and always have been a community. We are created in the image of God so we are created to live in community. Isolation is contrary to our design and God's will for our lives.

I was raised by two women and I felt shame in being different. I concluded that little girls grew up to be women, and most boys grew up to be men. But a few, like me, grew up to be monsters.

When I became an adult, I assumed that most men knew some secret man-club handshake or carried a man-card in their wallet. I knew that if I spent any time around them, they would discover I wasn't a real man, so I avoided close friendships with men whenever possible. I spent more time with women which served my lust addiction well.

Shame grew in me and it told me these messages:

1. If they knew the truth about me they would reject me.
2. I will never have my needs met by simply asking for help.
3. I am uniquely evil and beyond redemption.

These thoughts reflect my experience and are adapted from *Out of the Shadows* by Dr. Patrick Carnes. He writes that all sex addicts operate from a set of core beliefs.

1. Self-Image — I am basically a bad, unworthy person.
2. Relationships — No one would love me as I am.
3. Needs — My needs are never going to be met if I have to depend upon others.
4. Sexuality — Sex is my most important need.[26]

All of these messages have a common theme. Hide from others and live a secret life alone.

The solution to all of this is to live in community. Unfortunately, we addicts are convinced that community will kill us when it is, in fact, the very thing that will save us. Community is a healing place, but it requires the risk to be vulnerable and possibly even rejected. The best weapon against shame is community.

The Bible agrees. We are told the importance of confession. "If we confess our sins, he is faithful and just and will forgive us our sins and purify us from all unrighteousness" (1 John 1:9).

But Scripture also states, "Therefore, confess your sins to each other and pray for each other so that you may be healed. The prayer of a righteous person is powerful and effective" (James 5:16).

While we hold our sins and addictions in secret, healing is impossible. When we share our burdens with others in community, healing can happen.

In the first year of my recovery, I began to open up to other men for the first time in my life. After a while, I learned that telling the truth about who I was didn't cause other men to reject me. In fact, I learned to trust them and develop deeper relationships. I started sharing my heart in the safety of other recovering men and eventually, to friends and family who were not in recovery.

John Eldredge, in his book *Wild at Heart*,[27] makes the observation that masculinity is bestowed and can only come from other men. I wasn't conscious of it at the time, but in this company of other men, in community, I was beginning to become a man myself.

I am naturally an introvert, and in our marriage I would use my personality tendency as an excuse for not engaging in community. Robbie is much more social than me and one of her gifts is hospitality. I would use my antisocial behavior to undermine her gift and damage her soul. Recovery not only helped me open up to men, but it helped me appreciate and support Robbie's gifts.

Distrust vs. Gratitude

If you spend any time around 12 step groups or know people in them, you will hear the phrase "attitude of gratitude." Only two kinds of attitudes exist: gratitude and bad. Having an attitude of gratitude is about more than saying thank you when someone does something nice for you. It is based on the assumption that God and other people will do good things to and for you. The problem with that for me was that I wanted to be self-sufficient. Partly because of pride. Partly because of distrust.

What I discovered about myself was I assumed no good thing was ever going to come into my life that I didn't earn and work for. I expected nothing from anyone else or God. As a result, I believed I was in ultimate control. A byproduct of this belief was constant hurry. I was always rushing and never getting enough sleep. Hustle was the way to make sure good things happened.

As I grew in gratitude, I slowed down. I started driving the speed limit, not just with traffic but the actual speed limit. (Yes, I am *that* guy.) At the time, I was driving a retired police car so no one wanted to take the risk to pass me. It was fun to slow down everyone else.

I also committed myself to coming to a complete stop at every stop sign. I decided to purposely get into the longest line at the grocery store. I started getting more sleep and as it turns out, I was able to accomplish what needed to get done. Slowing down taught me to be at peace while trusting God.

Gratitude gradually became a way of life and in time I was able start trusting others, including Robbie.

While making these three changes—being present, living in community and practicing gratitude—I received the added gift of a healed and profoundly changed marriage. These principles are foundations of the Christian life. They have nothing, and yet everything, to do with addiction and recovery. They are about trust and living the way God intended. We always seem to struggle with the question of God's will for our lives. What if it is this simple? Live in the present, live in community and live in gratitude.

Chapter Thirteen

Laughter and the Beach

Maybe you and I were never meant to be complete,
Could we just be broken together?
—**Mark Hall**, from Casting Crowns "Broken Together"[28]

Robbie:

When I met John, his humor caused me to notice him and begin that wonderful, crazy, hot wheels track to falling in love. Every time we were together as we dated, we laughed. Even in the first seven years of lying to ourselves and each other, we always found ways to laugh. But during our eight months of painful reconciliation and recovery, we laughed very little.

Our God is good and knows that relationships need special ointment to treat the bruises and deep hurts. We were on our way to healing. We were growing individually in community with people who understood. We were talking. We were being honest. Now we needed a healing ointment to spur our recovery to completion.

It happened in the car.

Earlier that week, Betty and the group recommended I get an AIDS test. I told John I was thinking about this, and he assured me he'd not been with anyone. I didn't believe him.

"I've set an appointment with my doctor for next Thursday." I gritted my teeth in resolve.

"What for?"

"An AIDS test."

Silence.

"You don't have to do that, Robbie."

"Yes, I do, John. I have to take care of myself. You should probably get one yourself." Anger, our almost constant companion, was with us, sitting in the back seat. Again.

"What do I have to do, Robbie?"

"I don't know, John. You can't roll the clock back, can you?" We were on the verge of yelling.

"I just think this is unnecessary!"

"I think the man doth protest too much!"

We sat boiling and up ahead I noticed a billboard with a woman's face on it with the words "Have you seen this woman? Call 1-800-555-1212."

I blurted out, "I know what we should do. Let's take a picture of your "member" and put it up on a billboard with the question, 'Have you seen this? If so, call Robbie!'"

Silence.

Then John giggled. Just a little bit.

I joined him.

Soon we were laughing aloud so hard tears came to our eyes.

The wonderful ointment of God's grace fell into our car and started massaging our hearts. Laughter came back. It came with God's blessing. It came as an agent of healing. Through our laughter, I noticed Anger wasn't in the car with us anymore.

John reached out for my hand. I clasped his. It was the first touch of joy. (By the way, I got an AIDS test and demanded that John get one, too. They both came back negative.)

After eight months of celibacy and working diligently on our marriage, John and I decided to renew our vows. We chose a beach and invited twenty friends. Our home group, our best friends and some of the people in our therapy groups came to witness our renewal. The sun was shining, and the air smelled of sweet ocean water. I wore an off white flowing dress, satin and romantic. John wore his blue suit. I carried a bouquet of roses, and he wore a rose in his lapel. A good friend brought strawberries that we put on the rim of plastic champagne cups full of sparkling cider.

Unlike the frenetic wedding day years earlier, this occasion felt of peace. During the short ceremony, John and I exchanged vows. The meaning behind each word brought power to the promises. After what we'd been through, those few minutes of vowing our hearts and lives to each other became a worship ceremony to the God of all grace. After our second "I dos," our friends gathered around us, laid hands on us and prayed. That prayer sealed the deal. The family of believers who'd walked through the journey with us stood in the gap between the enemy and the Father and asked God to protect our union from attacks.

After the amens and hugs and tears shared throughout, we toasted, not each other but our friends and God. It was an offering of thanksgiving and praise. It reminded me of the verse where Joseph's brothers threw themselves down in remorse at Joseph's feet.

And Joseph said, "You intended to harm me, but God intended it for good…" Genesis 50:20

What Satan had intended to be yet another broken marriage, God restored.

After the ceremony, Noah went home with Gamma, and John and I had a nice dinner out and went home. As we turned in for the night, I thought of Daddy and the words he said to Mama before going to bed. We'd all be sitting watching TV or visiting and it would be time to hit the hay.

Daddy would announce, "Well, everybody, let's choose up sides and go to bed. Sally Ann, I choose you."

On that night after our renewal of vows, John and I chose each other. No one else was welcome in our bed anymore. No fantasies, no false idols and no lies of the enemy. Just us and the Spirit of God who blesses our union. We now consider our marriage bed a sacred place.

A couple of months after I'd left John, I attended my first writing conference. I'd been working on a novel for a few years, on and off, but I was a newcomer to the business. In fact, I knew nothing about how a book ever got published or even how to ask a magazine to consider an article. But it was time to do something I loved, just for me.

I registered for the writing conference at the last minute. When I arrived, I was instructed to sign up for a couple of one on one appointments with the staff.

Editors, agents and authors made up the faculty. I decided who I wanted to talk to. The big time keynote speaker was a best-selling author. I also wanted to talk to the agent that looked kind.

When I saw the big list on the wall, my heart fell. The only openings left were with a woman I'd never heard of. She was a pastor's wife who'd published some devotions. Great. An unknown writer. But she knew more than I did, so I wrote my name down.

The next day I went to her table where she was taking appointments.

"What are you writing?" She asked, using a common icebreaker for writers.

"A novel." I answered.

Then I started misting up. I am not sure what set it off, but suddenly I started crying out of the blue. Scarlet heat crept up my neck and face.

She didn't ask me what was wrong. I thought that was strange. She just sat there with this look of extreme compassion, soft and piercing.

"I don't know where this is coming from." I said, reaching for a tissue. They provided them for the appointments. Crying over your writing dreams is pretty common at these conferences. But I wasn't thinking about being published. I just felt pain over John.

"How is your marriage?"

Her question shocked me. I'd not said anything about our trouble. "Okay, I guess. We're working on it."

"May I pray for you?"

I agreed and she took both my hands in hers and we bowed our heads.

Again, she didn't say anything. I kept weeping, not all out bawling, but heavy tears of pain and release. She prayed silently. Then she spoke.

"God is giving me a picture for you." She dropped my hands and looked at me. "You and your husband were wild rivers before you met. Both of you were rushing waters, unsteady with no discipline, full of passion but no purpose."

She paused. My hands shook. She had read our mail.

"When you met, you joined rivers and became a huge wild river, shallow but with tremendous force. But then..." She paused again and I was frightened. Her words stabbed me with truth.

"But then something happened. God guided you to a waterfall and you both, as one wild rushing river, crashed off this waterfall. It hurt tremendously. And it was a gift from God."

I snorted, half crying and half chuckling. A gift? I didn't see it.

"God gave you such a wonderful gift. He will turn you both into a wonderful calm sea that is very, very deep. Peaceful and deep. Gorgeous and blue. And you will offer hope to others."

That wonderful woman gave me this prophecy thirteen years ago.

John has transformed from a man who was frightened, insecure and leading a double existence to a Godly man of integrity. God has given me the man I prayed for when I was young.

I am a woman who knows who she is in Christ. Insecurity still attacks me, but confidence has grown. Not because of anything I do or don't do, but because of God's power in my life. Through our story, God has humbled me and has given me a compassion for the many, many folks who follow Jesus but don't fit the "good Christian" mold.

John and I used to be addicted to drama – now we are addicted to contentment in God's will for us. We used to do everything we could to make sure others knew how much we loved God. Now we try to make sure those around us know that God loves them. We used to lie often, to ourselves and to each other. Now our home is a place where integrity is vital to our life. We used to feel hopelessness, scared that someone would discover who we really were. Now we live in hope, knowing that we are both fully known and fully loved by the Father.

We used to be raging rivers, out of control and desperately chasing God. Now we are a calm sea of peace, enjoying God's rays of sun and the refreshing splashes of His Spirit.

We are caught in the arms of a loving God.

Do's and Don'ts for a man (or woman) who might think he/she has a problem with pornography or an addiction to sex.

1. **Don't wait to get caught.** Instead reach out to get help from a pastor, counselor, and recovery fellowship. (See appendix for some national organizations)

2. **Don't believe the lies from shame and the enemy that everyone would be better off without you.** Addiction and suicide have a tragic link; don't let the enemy win by convincing you to kill yourself.

3. **Don't end your marriage for a better life with your affair partner.** You may believe the "grass is greener on the other side" but if you jump the fence you'll just kill another lawn. Stay in your marriage and learn how to have a thriving green lawn of your own.

4. **Do get help.** Recovery is like the famous line from the TV series *Lost*.[29] "We live together and we die alone." I have never seen anyone get real recovery trying to go it on their own. Recovery requires community and often professional help.

5. **Do tell your spouse everything.** Seek and follow the advice of your recovery fellowship and counselor on this. It is too easy to just dump your guilt on your spouse and leave them devastated. There are ways to do this and they almost always involve the help of others so it can be done in a way that will allow your marriage to survive. NOTE: Waiting to get caught eliminates the possibility of doing this well. Instead your spouse is devastated and you are caught in a lie that you may think you can continue.

Do's and Don'ts for a woman (or man) who might think she/he is married to a sex addict.

1. **Do remember the three Cs.** You didn't cause it, you can't control it and you can't cure it. Your spouse's addiction is not about you.

2. **Do pray and listen to your gut.** God has given each of us an internal intuition. Learn how to trust that intuition. If you feel something is going on with your husband, 95% of the time it is true. Sometimes it may be fear, but learn to distinguish between intuition and fear.

3. **Don't shame your husband into changing.** Honest confrontation is good and important but God changes hearts, not wives.

4. **Don't become a private investigator.** If you check email, texts, etc, you will just drive yourself crazy. If your husband wants to sin he will, whether you find out or not. (Refer to #1)

5. **Do decide what you can live with.** Get counsel and then draw a line in the sand. Divorce is your LAST OPTION. Always give you and your husband time to heal.

6. **Do look at yourself.** Use God's love, His Word and the counsel of professionals. You married this man. That means you have work to do on yourself.

Section Three:

CAUGHT IN THE ARMS
OF A LOVING GOD

(Or Ten Holy Habits that keep our Marriage Strong)

*If we don't change the direction we are headed we will certainly
end up where we are going.*
—Chinese Proverb[30]

Chapter Fourteen

Is There Hope?

"Be strong and take heart, all you who hope in the LORD"
(Psalm 31:24).

Robbie:

Brad and Jen, Blake and Miranda, Gwyneth and Chris and even Miss Piggy and Kermit. Divorce is such a prevalent practice in our society. Even the Muppets used it to be relevant and promote their TV show. (Even though the iconic pig and friendly frog were only dating—for 40 years.) How sad is that? And who cheated, Piggy or Kermit? Was it irreconcilable differences? I guess Kermit didn't turn out to be the frog-turned-prince she needed. And let's get real – Miss Piggy never, ever put Kermit first.

If you find yourself in a situation like ours, or any other couple who has a crisis, you will probably ask yourself the question we all do – Is there hope for my marriage?

John:

In my opinion, the answer is yes, with a qualifier.

Hope in Jesus

As a culture we use the word *hope* to mean "a desired positive outcome." We say things like "I hope you get well soon" or "I hope I get that promotion." That kind of hope has value but can wither under the heat of negative or undesirable circumstances. To have this kind of hope for your marriage can become meaningless when your spouse is unfaithful or unwilling to change hurtful behavior.

Instead, I'm talking about the way the word hope is used in the Bible. The Greek word means *expectation of what is sure* or put another way, hope in Jesus is a certainty.

I liken it to an anchor on a ship. The idea is that a ship in a harbor can be pushed by wind and current and be destroyed on the rocks. The ship is powerless to resist these forces and will certainly be lost. But the sailors, knowing this, drop anchor so the ship is held in place and is safe. The sailors don't simply arrive and "hope" the wind won't push the ship onto the rocks; they take action and use the anchor.

In this situation, the anchor is not the hope. The hope is that the sea floor is stronger than the wind. You see the wind is stronger than the ship and can push it across the water, but it is not stronger than the sea floor. So the anchor is not the point or the source of strength. What matters is the object of the hope or what you place your hope in.

"...we who have fled to take hold of the hope set before us may be greatly encouraged. We have this hope as an anchor for the soul, firm and secure..." (Hebrews 6:18-19).

Ten Holy Habits

This next section of the book is an unapologetic assertion that Jesus is the only real hope for a broken marriage.

We list ten holy habits that we practice and that will point you and your spouse to Him as well as strengthen your connection to Him.

The sailors needed to do more than simply believe dropping the anchor would secure the ship. That belief alone was meaningless until they took the actions necessary to set the anchor in the sea floor so the hope was secure.

If you follow these ten holy habits we have learned and "set anchor" in Jesus, He alone can save your marriage.

A thought to consider—Robbie and I were Christians and committed Christ followers when our marriage fell apart. This might be true for you as well. One of the things I have learned about sin is that it carries an often unconsidered consequence of forgetfulness. We learn about living with Jesus and as a result, our identity in Christ becomes a defining quality for our life. But we all too often forget about that identity and revert to those negative thoughts which leave us separated from God. We then run to those things we think might keep us safe that are less than God and by definition idols. It is necessary that we learn disciplines to keep connected with Jesus. If you practice these ten holy habits you will stay connected to Jesus, and therefore, your marriage will thrive. Consistent habits solve the problem of forgetting. You can stay connected to Jesus, your source, and through these habits become connected to your spouse in a way that has probably eluded you so far.

It will be hard work, but if our experience is any indicator, that work will be rewarded over and over.

We invite you now to let go of false hope and instead start the work of setting your hope in Jesus.

Robbie and I have a cheer that goes,

"Jesus, Jesus, He's our man,

if He can't do it, we're all going to Hell."

This may not reflect your sense of humor, but it is none the less, true. When we place our hope in anything other than Jesus, like good works, or church attendance, we cannot be saved. The same is true for your marriage. This is not a "self-help book." This is a "my-marriage-is-drowning-and-if-Jesus-doesn't-rescue-it-there-is-no-hope-book."

Our ten holy habits are not the only way; Jesus is the only way and these habits are a way of setting the anchor for your marriage in Him so the wind and waves don't leave your marriage shipwrecked. It is our prayer that the Father would give you peace and would strengthen your faith in Him.

Chapter Fifteen

Die to Yourself that Your Marriage Might Live

In marriage, the goal is holiness, not happiness.
—Erwin Lutzer[31]

John:

On the wall of our bedroom, a painting hangs that was created by a high school student from Albuquerque, New Mexico. It shows a woman, faceless, slightly bending down. Seeds drop from her and out of her back grows a big sunflower. The verse at the bottom of the painting is "Very truly I tell you, unless a kernel of wheat falls to the ground and dies, it remains only a single seed. But if it dies, it produces many seeds" (John 12:24).

Robbie's brother Phil gave her this painting after we moved to Denver. She was having a difficult time adjusting to our new life, especially the cold, after twenty years in beautiful San Diego. This painting reminds us we are to die to ourselves. Because of the supernatural Spirit we serve, death will lead to life. This is true in marriage. We must die to our self-centeredness and our selfish desires.

Difficult, but doable.

After the day we renewed our vows on the beach, our marriage was perfect.

Um, no. Of course not. But having lived without each other emotionally and having fought for our marriage, we were ready to do whatever it took to make our marriage the best it could be. We consciously and intentionally died to our own idea of what our marriage "should" fulfill in us. We put into place new behaviors. Some we learned in our months of counseling. We developed a few out of our trial and error experience.

Establish the bottom line — Covenant vs. Contract

First, we agreed that our marriage is not a contract but a covenant. When we first married, we agreed to love each other as long as the other person held up their end of the deal. That arrangement was not in the vows, but it was our underlying pact. This is a pervasive philosophy in our culture that goes hand in hand with "if it feels good, do it." A recent survey reported that 40% of millennials believe the words "til death do us part" should be omitted from the marriage vows.[32] But for a marriage to thrive and grow as God wants it to, we must die to ourselves and remember that our marriage is a covenant, not a contract.

According to Dave Willis, co-founder of StrongerMarriages.org, there are seven distinctions between a covenant marriage and contract:[33]

Covenant Marriage vs Contract Marriage

1. In a covenant marriage, you'll be focused on your spouse's rights. In a contract marriage, you'll be focused on your own rights.

2. In a covenant marriage, you choose to love and respect your spouse even when they don't "deserve it." In a contract marriage, you are free to give your spouse the treatment you believe he or she deserves.

3. In a covenant marriage, there's no "escape clause." In a contract marriage, divorce is always an option.

4. In a covenant marriage, there's no keeping score of each other's mistakes. In a contract marriage, there's no forgetting each other's mistakes.

5. In a covenant marriage, couples work with mutual respect through disagreement. In contract marriages, individuals try to "win" the argument against their spouse.

6. In a covenant marriage, couples believe their marriage is primarily about serving. In a contract marriage, couples believe marriage is about getting.

7. In a covenant marriage, couples believe their marriage is a sacred partnership. In contract marriages, couples believe their relationship is a legal partnership.

Couples who know God is the foundation of their bond are usually more likely to work through challenges together. If you believe your marriage is nothing more than a legal document, chances are much greater you'll eventually have another legal document called a certificate of divorce.

Borrow a Cup of Faith

Robbie:

Before beginning to develop habits to energize and protect your marriage, consider finding someone who has faith in and for your marriage, and borrow that faith. It is easy to get to a point where your relationship feels hopeless. You've tried talking and nothing is resolved. Too much hurt or betrayal divides you. Maybe you've even tried counseling, but to no avail. You are not the only one who has ever gone through this kind of pain. "Resist him, standing firm in the faith, because you know that the family of believers throughout the world is undergoing the same kind of sufferings" (1 Peter 5:9). You are not alone.

Someone else might have the hope you need. Finding that hope might begin with finding another person/couple who has hope for your marriage. For us, Doug and Betty, our individual counselors, gave us hope. The fellow strugglers in our groups who were further along in the journey had faith when we had none. And our friends Jeff and Theresa took this position. They loved us and prayed for us and loaned us their faith. They didn't take sides. Find someone in your life to intercede in prayer for your marriage. Someone to take you to Jesus when you have no energy left.

John:

Earlier I told the story about relying on the faith of Doug and my fellow recovering sex addicts during counseling. Just like those friends carried me, find friends who can carry your marriage to Jesus while you are healing. Someday you will do the same for another couple. This is vital, not just a good idea. Working to improve your marriage can be a struggle, and it is easy to lose hope. If you are convinced that your faith alone is sufficient, the only option will be a divorce when the situation exceeds your faith. Relying on the faith of others is a safety net you must have for your marriage to survive.

1 Corinthians 13

Robbie:

A common reading at weddings is 1 Corinthians 13. It's almost a cliché, since it is repeated so often when marriage is discussed. However, it is not as common for a married couple to live out these verses in every aspect of their relationship. It definitely was not the case in our marriage. After our wedding, as we adjusted to living together, self-centeredness grew, not love. I think that since we had the rings and the license and we'd made the commitment, I assumed that love would grow. But love doesn't grow by itself. It needs nourishment and tending. It isn't a natural outpouring of marriage, just because we got married. It is a conscious choice. It is work.

1 Corinthians 13 tells us what love is and what it does. Have you thought about what love does *not do*?

Love does not:

1. Abuse you, deny abuse, intimidate with threats or anger.
2. Call you names, embarrass you with put downs.
3. Control what you see, do or talk to.
4. Ask you to change who you are at your core.
5. Make all the decisions.
6. Resent your success.
7. Give up on you or the marriage.
8. Discourage your growth.

If you are in a marriage where any of these things occur, you both need to work on your marriage or get help to heal your marriage. These actions are not love.

John:

"Above all, love each other deeply, because love covers over a multitude of sins" (1 Peter 4:8). This kind of love is an action more than a feeling. In 1 Corinthians 13, we get a 16 point working definition of love.

This is what love is:

1. Love is Patient
2. Love is Kind
3. Love Does Not Envy
4. Love Does Not Boast

5. Love is Not Proud

6. Love Does Not Dishonor Others (Love Honors Others)

7. Love is Not Self-Seeking

8. Love is Not Easily Angered

9. Love Keeps No Record of Wrongs

10. Love Does Not Delight in Evil

11. Love Rejoices in the Truth

12. Love Always Protects

13. Love Always Trusts

14. Love Always Hopes

15. Love Always Perseveres

16. Love Never Fails

So what does this kind of love look like in marriage?

Robbie and I like to take road trips. Our normal modus operandi is I drive and Robbie navigates. Occasionally we will switch. Travelling together in a car is a common scenario where married couples have ample opportunity to love their spouse, but also many chances to not practice love. Robbie and I can easily get into petty fights in the car.

"Go that way." Robbie will say.

"What is that way?" I will respond in annoyance.

"The right!"

Of course, at this point I have missed the turn and begin to blame my lovely wife's inability to be specific.

When she is driving:

"Be careful because there are two teenagers crossing the road up there." I'll encourage.

"I can see them, John."

"Remember that you want to go left up here so get in the left hand turn lane."

"I know how to drive, John!!'

For some unknown reason, she's now annoyed with me.

In our marriage, it's difficult to distinguish between being the navigator or aggravator.

Love is patient, kind and not easily angered. Driving with our cherished spouse is a great opportunity to practice 1 Corinthians 13 love.

Robbie:

And what about those old tunes of blame that reoccur in your home like a radio station that can't seem to find any new songs? Those moments where your spouse will once again, leave clothes on the floor or lose the keys or forget to turn the lights off. The annoying songs of bad habits that at first are simply inconvenient. But after a while, they irritate you like an owl screeching in the dead of night.

Love doesn't keep a record of wrongs. It perseveres with gentleness. I have this annoying habit of leaving my empty fake sugar packets on the counter after I make my coffee in the morning. John asked me about it at first and I told him I would try to throw them away. The next time, John threw them away in front of me while locking eyes with mine. Message received.

"Oops." I said with a grin, telling myself I'd get better.

Then it happened again. And again.

After exacting his revenge, John went to jail for a while.

Just kidding! He reminded me again gently. He persevered. It could've gotten ugly. I finally learned how to pick up the green and white packet and put it in the trash. Voila! Love won out!

Loving your spouse like Jesus tells us to love is much like pushing a boulder up a hill. In our society, if you are not actively and intentionally loving your spouse, the boulder (your marriage) will roll back downhill. It is, as my mom put it, "The hardest job you will ever love." We've met many couples who are having problems in their marriage simply because they are not *working* to love each other in 1 Corinthian 13 ways.

Bob Goff wrote a wonderful book titled *Love Does: Discover a Secret Incredible Life in an Ordinary World*.[34] In it, he makes an observation that if Paul heard, he might say "Add it to the 1 Corinthians 13 list."

Bob writes "love is never stationary."

Our Five Overarching Principles for our Ten Habits:

Your Spouse is the one you CHOSE so CHOOSE to love them.

It's Gonna Hurt but it's worth it.

Your Spouse is a Unique Gift from God, not your Enemy.

It's Time to Let Go of your Wedding-Day Expectations and be Married to your *Actual* Spouse.

When you Married, God had a Plan for you as a Couple. Live in it.

The 10 Holy Habits

H—Handle Your Marriage with Prayer.

O—Own YOUR Role – Go First.

L—Launch true Intimacy by Confession.

Y—You Build Trust through Forgiveness.

H—Honor her/him with your words.

A—Accept responsibility and Fight Fair.

B—Break the Need for Control.

I—Ignite the Individuality in your Spouse.

T—Team up for God's Purposes.

S—Sow Laughter and Reap Joy.

1st Overarching Principle –

Your Spouse is the one you CHOSE so CHOOSE to love them.

*He loved her of course, but better than that,
he chose her, day after day.
Choice: that was thing.*
—Sherman Alexie[35]

Chapter Sixteen

Habit #1 – Handle Your Marriage with Prayer

Many things I have tried to grasp and have lost. That which I have placed in God's hands I still have.

—Martin Luther[36]

Robbie:

My one pregnancy was extremely difficult. I was overweight and 36 years old. I had gestational diabetes and toxemia. I was grumpy and strung out on hormones all the time. During month eight, one of the teachers I worked with told me, "Robbie, you are a poster child for birth control." Normally, I would've been insulted, but she spoke truth and I laughed out loud. By the time Noah was due, everyone was ready for his arrival and a possible return to sanity for me.

After 36 hours of labor, complete with drugs to help me not stroke out due to eclampsia, I had a C-Section and we all welcomed Noah Walker Iobst into the world. I was on some fabulous drugs so John held up Noah to my face and I introduced myself and kissed him. I was deliriously happy.

Then he coughed. Or what sounded like a tiny cough.

Soon, I was abandoned with just one doctor and one nurse. The other doctors and nurses skedaddled out of the room with John in tow. I was told that they needed to check out Noah and to not worry. I was sky high and told the gay orderly I loved him several times.

John:

My world flipped upside down in matter of seconds. I was expecting the words "Let's weigh your son" but instead someone took him out of my arms and said, "Come with us." I followed a line of medical professionals in urgency.

The next minutes seemed like days. I saw more doctors, nurses and medical equipment surround my son than I had seen in my entire life. It was the worst version of a medical television show and all I could do was watch. After some time, two doctors wanted me to sign one of two sets of consent forms to treat Noah's hyper-pulmonary tension. The first form would put Noah on a heart-lung bypass machine which was the standard of care for his condition. The second was to approve treatment with an experimental drug that this hospital was using as a trial. One of the doctors explained that he was running the trial and that Noah was an excellent candidate for the new treatment protocol. He explained the positive results he'd seen in newborns. So with my son less than an hour old and my wife in recovery from the C-Section, I trusted the doctor and signed Noah up for an experimental treatment. I didn't sleep much that night.

Robbie:

As soon as John told me about Noah being in the NICU, (Neonatal Intensive Care Unit) I prayed and then started calling prayer warriors.

Over the next few days, little by little Noah seemed to improve. I spent all the time I could with him, even though I wasn't able to hold him.

On day four I was discharged. That night John and I left the hospital without a baby. It was devastating, even though we knew Noah was making good progress. When we got home, I fell on the bed and began to sob. John joined me and held me, gently rubbing my back. At one point, I looked at him and saw tears on his face. It was just as devastating to him.

Pray because you are Desperate

The most natural thing in the world at that moment was to pray. We were desperate and the Father loves prayers of desperation. We prayed for our baby boy for healing, for no permanent damage and for our Lord to carry us through.

"If my people, who are called by my name, will humble themselves and pray and seek my face and turn from their wicked ways, then I will hear from heaven, and I will forgive their sin and will heal their land" (2 Chronicles 7:14).

I prayed these words like never before.

The definition of the word *desperate* is "losing all hope."[37]

God loves desperate prayers because He gets a chance to help us and show off His glory. When Jesus healed, He responded to desperate people and desperate cries.

In Mark 5:25-34, the woman who had been bleeding for years said, "If I just touch His clothes, I will be healed." The Bible tells us that she said this to herself, but Jesus heard her cry and her desperation and He healed her.

In Luke 17:11-19, the ten lepers yelled out to Jesus, "Have pity on us!" He healed them all and yet only one of those desperate lepers came to thank Him.

And in Matthew 20:30-34 two blind men yelled to Jesus, "Have mercy on us!" Jesus asked them the question He asks all of us, "What do you want me to do for you?" They replied, "We want our sight."

Imagine if Jesus asked you right now, "What do you want me to do for your marriage?" Answer with desperation and faith.

We left the hospital with Noah on his fifteenth day of life. Happy and blessed and nervous about the new baby, we went home and once again, fell on the bed. This time, there were three of us.

Pray because you are Grateful

The most natural thing in the world to do at that moment was to pray a prayer of thanksgiving. We were desperately grateful, and the Father loves prayers of gratitude.

> *Here are the two best prayers I know: Help me, help me, help me'*
> *and 'thank you, thank you, thank you.*
> **—Anne Lamott** [38]

As Noah grew up healthy, we continued to say thank you. We tried to put the Word into practice. "Give thanks to the Lord for He is good; His love endures forever" (1 Chronicles 16:34). When I watched Noah learn to crawl and walk, I remembered the Lord's enduring love. John and I memorized "Give thanks in all circumstances; for this is God's will for you in Christ Jesus" (1 Thessalonians 5:18).

Out of our gratitude, praying became a habit for us. Each night, we would pray. Our prayers always began with "Father, thank You." Praying before we went to bed became as natural to us as brushing teeth. Over the next four years, we prayed most every night. It was just one of the things we did every day.

Then I left John. Our world blew up.

Divorce, instead of a word never spoken in our home, was whispered in both of our hearts. John agreed to the list of requirements that our counselor Doug and I made. I came home. With me came a tsunami of anger. On the first night I was home, I was determined that we should pray like we'd always done.

"We have to do this," I told John. I said it in anger, with an underlying attack that insinuated *if you prayed like a real Christian, we wouldn't be here.* John acquiesced and we prayed short, insincere prayers of anger and shame. Eventually God told me to shut up about anything spiritual and we prayed rarely, if ever.

But towards the end of our reconciliation period, we began to pray consistently again and our prayers changed. Instead of words of gratitude, our prayers of desperation were uttered in our bedroom each night. John began to pray, "Please rescue our marriage." I heard humility in John's voice and I joined in and we both became anxious for God to do *something. Anything.*

He did, indeed, rescue us.

John:

Even when we prayed in anger or shame or apathy, God saw we were looking to Him. He answered. And the habit of praying together ushered in a new season of honesty.

Pray to Reinforce Honesty in Your Marriage

In Psalm 18, David talks about feeling "the torments of destruction" around him. That describes our marriage. Then David goes on to cry out to God for help. God hears and "parted the heavens and came down. He mounted the cherubim and flew. He soared on the wings of the wind" (Psalm 18:9-10).

When Robbie and Noah drove away from our home on that horrible night, my son prayed for me in a short simple sentence, "God, please help Daddy."

God heard my boy and He soared on the wings of the wind to help.

Psalm 18:16-17 says "He reached down from on high and pulled me out of deep waters. He rescued me from my enemies, from my foes who were too strong for me...."

We asked and God rescued us. When you pray to be rescued, your prayer keeps you honest and humbled in front of God and your spouse. We knew each other inside and out and attempting any sort of lie or show in prayer would be futile. We both knew that.

Mark Merrill with the Family Minute put it perfectly—"The act of prayer— hand-in-hand, quiet, focused, on our knees, with heads bowed keeps us in a position of openness and humility. We are engaged in an act of worship. We are showing our reverence for God and each other. It's hard to be judgmental and argumentative when you're in that stance."[39]

We don't have rules around our prayers. Some nights, we pray short prayers and go to sleep. Some nights, one of us has a lot to pray and the other, very little. We don't judge each other's prayers. We don't try to sound super spiritual. We know each other too well.

And although we've done this before, we don't use prayer to preach to each other. In the past, Robbie used prayers like this in front of me. "Father, thank You for John. Please teach him how to listen to me when I am anxious and teach him to reflect Your love for me when he is watching football." Not anymore.

I don't pray, "Father thank you for Robbie. Help her learn to stop talking." No prayers like this. I mean, come on, I value my life.

We just pray. Every night, or as consistently as we can.

Pray to Save Your Marriage

You may have observed that even after praying together every night for four years, Robbie left me. Our marriage crashed. So prayer didn't do anything, right? Wrong. I think in asking God to be a part of our household, we were giving Him permission to root out the evil. And He did. God rescued our marriage because we cried out for help. And we kept on crying out together. It is difficult to pray with your spouse when you feel anger toward them. It can be worse when you feel nothing. But we did it, and we believe our marriage was saved because we asked God to be a part of our family every day.

As we prayed, God began changing our hearts toward each other and Him. Hope was born in a tiny cottage in Lemon Grove, California simply because we chose to pray together every day.

We believe that praying together saved our marriage. The National Association of Marriage Enhancement, in Phoenix, Arizona reported that when couples prayed together on a daily basis, far less than 1% of those couples would end up getting a divorce.[40]

Dr. David Stoop wrote, "Unfortunately, not very many Christian couples read the Bible together or pray together. The number I've heard is that only about 4% of Christian couples pray together on a daily basis. The reason might be related to the fact that not many pastoral couples pray together daily. Their percentage is only about 6%. The important take-away is that if you want to strengthen your marriage—and even "divorce-proof" your marriage—develop a consistent pattern of reading the Bible together and praying together in your home."[41]

According to a study by AARP—some shocking statistics: while 50% of first marriages end in divorce, and 78% of second marriages end in divorce, less than 1% of couples who pray together daily end their marriages.[42]

Prayer works. It is the secret, the special sauce and the number one key to saving a marriage.

Pray to Grow Your Marriage

Robbie:

As we have grown in our relationship to God and each other, we now believe that prayer is not just for desperation, gratitude, honesty and rescuing. We believe that prayer grows us and guides us.

We pray about our teenage boy and our girls and grand-girls. We pray about our jobs and ministry. We pray for supernatural guidance. God steers our lives because we ask Him.

Pray as though your marriage is a God-sized problem that you alone cannot manage.

I believe dreaming big dreams and praying big prayers for your marriage makes God giggle. He gets to show off because we ask. The best part of God-sized problems and dreams is that we have a God-sized God who can solve them and make them happen.

In his fantastic book *The Circle Maker*, Mark Batterson writes, "Prayers are prophecies. They are the best predictors of your spiritual future. Who you become is determined by how you pray. Ultimately, the transcript of your prayers becomes the script of your life."[43]

Prayer works. To have a fulfilling marriage, making prayer a habit is vital.

Chapter Seventeen

Habit #2–
Own Your Role—Go First!

Sometimes in my own marriage I've been frustrated by my husband's supposed selfishness, only to realize that it is me who needs the attitude adjustment. Once I begin to look inside myself at what is really going on, I can get back on the road to becoming the selfless person my partner deserves.

—Tudie Rose[44]

John:

When I think of the words "go first" my mind always goes to that famous scene in *Raiders of the Lost Ark*. Indiana Jones opens the Well of the Souls chamber and looks down.

Sallah: Indy, why does the floor move?

Indiana: Give me your torch.

(He drops the torch down to the ground)

Indiana: Snakes. Why'd it have to be snakes?

Sallah: Asps...very dangerous. You go first.[45]

Who would want to go first in that situation? In marriage, we may not come across a chamber of poisonous snakes, but in many circumstances we want our spouse to be the first to delve in and sacrifice.

But in the context of our marriage, "Go first!" is all about serving, which is the essence of love. In Matthew 20, Jesus told the parable of the workers and He ended His story with "So the last will be first, and the first will be last." In the same chapter, the mother of James and John asked Jesus if her sons could sit on His right and left in the kingdom of God. Jesus told her and her boys no. When the other disciples found out, they became indignant. So in Matthew 20:26-28 Jesus told them all, "Whoever wants to become great among you must be your servant, and whoever wants to be first must be your slave— just as the Son of Man did not come to be served, but to serve, and to give his life as a ransom for many."

When we talk about going first, we are talking about being *the first to serve the other*.

Go First in Obedience

Many sermons on marriage focus on these verses: "Wives, submit yourselves to your own husbands as you do to the Lord. For the husband is the head of the wife as Christ is the head of the church, his body, of which he is the Savior. Now as the church submits to Christ, so also wives should submit to their husbands in everything. Husbands, love your wives, just as Christ loved the church and gave himself up for her to make her holy, cleansing her by the washing with water through the word, and to present her to himself as a radiant church, without stain or wrinkle or any other blemish, but holy and blameless. In this same way, husbands ought to love their wives as their own bodies. He who loves his wife loves himself" (Ephesians 5:22-28).

Essentially, Paul is asking wives to respect their husbands and husbands to love their wives.

Our selfishness, our carnal nature, tells us to look out for number one. This relationship is about *me* so I need to have my needs met. I need Robbie to respect me. If and when she respects me, *then* I will love her. In the same way, wives decide that they will respect their husbands deeply, *once* they feel loved.

But God is asking you and me to **go first**. Be the first to respect, even when you feel unloved. Be the first to love, even when you feel disrespected. The idea is to think of love as an action not a feeling, and as such, it is subject to our wills. I decide to drive my car; I don't simply find myself driving because of a feeling I had no choice over. Going first means that I will take the actions of love **before** my spouse does something that makes me feel like she deserves it. That means I need to love Robbie even if she does not act respectfully to me, or if I don't feel she has done anything deserving of love. Likewise, Robbie needs to respect me even I haven't first loved her, and even when I have not done anything deserving of respect. We each need to focus on obeying God, not simply doing what we consider fair.

Marriage is not a contract and one of the best ways for me to live in a covenant is to take the actions of love when it is not fair. When it comes to love...Go First!

Going First as an Act of the Will

Robbie:

In our early marriage, I desperately wanted to respect John. So much so, that I made the choice to be his public relations representative, telling everyone how wonderful he was. But in my heart, I didn't respect him. I wanted him to love me like I was a princess, his beautiful bride, but I felt that he loved himself more than me. So I was an example of public vs. private. In public, I told everyone that John was this incredible Christian spiritual leader. In private, I disrespected him in word and action, because he didn't love me like I thought Christ loved the church.

After our reconciliation, I worked hard to become an authentic person, without two personas, the pubic and the private. I also decided to *go first as an act of my will.* I chose to respect John and the work he was doing for his sobriety and all the areas of his life affected. It was a decision. An act of the will, like getting out of bed in the morning. I went first because it was the right thing to do, even though it didn't always feel good.

John:

Early in our marriage I used "love" as a way to get what I wanted and regularly withheld it to try to force Robbie to respect me. Sometimes I used "not loving" simply to punish her for not being my version of the perfect wife. In my recovery, I learned to be honest with myself and Robbie and started taking the act of loving my wife seriously. I came to understand that God wanted me to love Robbie not because it was fair or I felt like it, but because we are one flesh and loving her was meeting her deep and God-given need. Honoring God and Robbie was setting me free. My addiction was about trying to feel loved. I started to understand that by giving love and placing Robbie first, I was able to experience God's love for me in a deeper way than I thought was possible. Just another paradox of Christianity—if you want to live, die. If you want to be loved, love first even if it doesn't feel fair.

"For whoever wants to save their life will lose it, but whoever loses their life for me and for the gospel will save it" (Mark 8:35).

In marriage, if you don't make it a habit to go first, your marriage will suffer and/or die.

Going First Strategically

John:

According to Gary Chapman's book *The Five Love Languages*, each of us feel the most loved when someone communicates love through our love language:

1) acts of service, 2) quality time, 3) words of affirmation, 4) physical affection and 5) gifts.[46]

For example, Trevor might have the love language of quality time. If his wife, Becky, knows this, then she can make sure to intentionally and strategically spend time with Trevor. In making that effort, she is loving him in a way he feels the most loved. On the other hand, Becky's love language is physical affection. If Trevor knows this, he can intentionally and strategically make sure to hold her hand while they are walking or give her back rubs, just so she can feel loved.

One way to go first in your marriage is to love your spouse by learning his/her love language. Learning and acting in the others' love language is important so that love is effective and can be felt.

Part of going first is accepting, without criticism, your spouse's halting attempts at expressing love in your native language. Since it is not their own, they won't do it as well as you would, but it is important for you to rejoice in the attempt.

The next part of going first is dying to the right of only accepting love from my spouse in my love language. For example, Trevor can accept that when Becky gives him a back rub, it is an expression of her love. She is acting in her love language. Becky can acknowledge that when Trevor asks to take a walk and just be together, he is loving her in his love language.

Changing to the other's love language needs to be a choice, not a requirement, or it is simply another form of a contract and not really love at all.

I know for Robbie, spending time over a meal talking and listening says I love her more than me serving her. Her love language is words of affirmation. But mine is service. Robbie has come to appreciate and applaud my native love language of service when I do the laundry or fill her car up with gas. Love languages go both ways. To go first in your marriage strategically is to:

- Learn to love your spouse in their love language.
- Learn to accept the way your spouse loves you, even if it is not your love language.

Doing both of these might seem contradictory. So let me be clear. Going first means that you do both and at the same time require neither from your spouse.

Robbie:

I have always wanted John to use his words to tell me I was brilliant and beautiful. (The more often, the better.) He used to do this occasionally, but he made a point of serving me in all sorts of little ways. I thought that was kind, but I wanted him to affirm me with his words. In the same way, I told John all the time how wonderful he was. But I didn't serve him consistently.

I've now learned that when John fills up my car with gas, it is his way of saying, "You are wonderful and I love you." But he also makes an attempt to tell me, too. As for me, I still affirm his wonderful traits with words, but I also try to serve him in ways he will feel loved.

Case in point is our microwave. I don't really mind if it is a bit dirty. (I can be a bit of a slob.) I've learned, though, that John really enjoys it clean. He insists that the microwave works better if it is clean. I am not sure that's true, but it makes him happy so I go along with it. So if I take time to clean out the microwave, he beams when he discovers my act of service. It's like the "ding!" when the food is ready. Ding! John feels loved.

We recommend Gary Chapman's *The Five Love Languages* highly. Invest in your marriage and buy a copy.

Going first in obedience, as an act of the will and strategically will save your marriage from a heap of heartache. Or a chamber of asps.

2ⁿᵈ Overarching Principle –

It's Gonna Hurt,
but it's Worth It!

It's supposed to be hard. If it wasn't hard, everyone would do it. The hard is what makes it great.
—Jimmy Dugan to Dottie Hinson
in *A League of their Own.* [47]

Chapter Eighteen

Habit #3 – Launch True Intimacy by Practicing Confession

The difficult thing is that vulnerability is the first thing I look for in you and the last thing I'm willing to show you. In you, it's courage and daring. In me, it's weakness.
—Brene Brown.[48]

Robbie:

It was a beautiful home in Del Mar, California and everyone looked beautiful. A woman I worked with was getting married and we were having a wedding shower. All the food was tiny and the flowers matched and I could feel the estrogen bouncing off the walls. I loved it.

We gathered together in the living room in a semi-circle to ooh and aah as the bride-to-be opened her presents. Her first gift was a lovely negligee. The next, a teddy. The third one she opened was some panties and a bra.

"Hmm." I whispered to the lady who sat beside me. "She is getting a lot of lingerie, isn't she?"

My friend looked at me. "Robbie didn't you read the invitation?"

My heart skipped. Uh-oh.

"This is a lingerie shower."

I thought about faking a coughing attack and leaving but I decided to be brave.

"This is from Robbie," she said happily, as she got to my gift. She was gracious and hid her immediate shock when she saw what it was. "Oh, I registered for this."

All eyes were on her as she held up my gift—an electric knife.

Not exactly spice up the night material, right?

As I was leaving, one woman approached me and said as she giggled, "There's nothing like an electric knife for intimacy."

I laughed along with her. I often embarrass myself so I wasn't shocked at my mistake. But I did wonder about the use of the word 'intimacy' by this woman. Did she equate intimacy with sex? Through our work with marriages, we've found most people of both sexes do.

But in the rebuilding of our marriage, it became crucial for me to realize that intimacy and sex are not the same thing.

What is Intimacy?

John:

Intimacy is difficult. But when we achieve real intimacy it makes the marriage great. Intimacy is "being completely honest about your thoughts, feelings and actions." I've heard some say that intimacy is "Into Me, See."

God's perfect plan included intimacy with all of us. In the garden of Eden God shared intimacy with Adam and Eve. In fact, He set up a three dimensional flesh and blood metaphor for what intimacy with Him looks like.

"The man said, 'This is now bone of my bones and flesh of my flesh; she shall be called 'woman' for she was taken out of man.' That is why a man leaves his father and mother and is united to his wife and they become one flesh. Adam and his wife were both naked, and they felt no shame" (Genesis 2:23-25).

In this passage, the whole leave and cleave thing seemed out of place to me. Adam and Eve had no father or mother so how could they understand what this meant? But it was important enough for Jesus to repeat it twice in Matthew and Mark.

"Haven't you read," he (Jesus) replied, "that at the beginning the Creator 'made them male and female,' and said, 'For this reason a man will leave his father and mother and be united to his wife, and the two will become one flesh'" (Matthew 19:4-5)?

"But at the beginning of creation God 'made them male and female.' 'For this reason a man will leave his father and mother and be united to his wife, and the two will become one flesh.' So they are no longer two, but one flesh. Therefore, what God has joined together, let no one separate" (Mark 10:7).

One Flesh, One Intimacy

In Ephesians 5, Paul pulls out his powerful apostle decoder ring and explains what this seemingly out of place statement really means. Paul teaches on the church as the body of Christ.

"...for we are members of his body. 'For this reason a man will leave his father and mother and be united to his wife and the two will become one flesh.' This is a profound mystery—but I am talking about Christ and the church" (Ephesians 5:30-32).

So the leaving and cleaving, one flesh union, naked and not ashamed language is a metaphor for the kind of intimate relationship God wants with His children. That kind of relationship was lost in the fall and replaced with shame, covering up, lying and blaming others. If you think about it, it is the perfect metaphor. When in our lives are we more vulnerable, more exposed and at the same time more loved and safe than when we are in a one flesh union with our spouse?

We lost intimacy with God in the fall, and we traded it for shame when Adam and Eve sinned. Their first emotion after sin – shame. "Then the eyes of both of them were opened, and they realized they were naked: so they sewed fig leaves together and made coverings for themselves" (Genesis 3:7).

Shame blocked Adam and Eve from having that perfect familiarity with God. Shame blocks a husband or wife from having a real heart to heart relationship with his/her spouse.

So how do we practice intimacy with our spouse? How do we get rid of any shame that might be between us? We are called to be completely crushingly honest with our spouse and God.

Image Management Blocks Intimacy

Robbie:

On that bay in San Diego during our furniture moving sessions, John took on some of the burdens I was fighting, and I took some of his. In sharing our fears and secrets, intimacy happened. Although I was angry, I was also relieved and glad we were finally being completely honest with one another. Some of the things he told me I will never repeat. But as any woman will tell you, I wanted the truth most of all, no matter how ugly it was. Because then I was able to process it. You can't deal with someone else's secret, but your life can be altered by it. Honesty is always better, no matter how much pain it creates.

Of course, I needed to be completely honest with John. I have had times when I've not told John about a bill or a receipt, simply because I didn't want to make him angry or disappoint him. I felt shame. When I do this I am blocking intimacy. At times I haven't told John the honest truth because I didn't want to hurt him. Again, I am blocking intimacy. I want John to look at me as this perfect wife who has her spending habits completely in check and who is all knowing and wise, even when I am not. I practice what John calls "image management."

John:

I was about six months into recovery when I got a full time job at a telecom company. As part of my addiction, I was either unemployed or under employed for years and that placed an unreasonable burden on Robbie. My weekly group therapy met each Wednesday night so my work schedule allowed me to have each Thursday off. Robbie was teaching at the time and worked Monday through Friday each week.

On the Thursday of each week I was home alone and I used the time to process the group session the night before and to do the family laundry. At the time we lived in a rental home that didn't have a washer/drier but the landlord who lived next door allowed us to use theirs. Thursdays were good for laundry, because they weren't using it at the time.

As I was doing the laundry one day, we ran out of detergent so I used some of the landlord's. They were not there to give me permission, but we would just replace what was used.

That night when Robbie came home she noticed the laundry was done.

"John, how did you do the laundry? Aren't we out of detergent?"

My borrowing the landlord's detergent was not an issue at all and that makes the next few moments all the more disturbing.

"We had just enough to get the laundry done." I lied.

If addiction has a "native tongue" it would be lying. But this was more complicated than that. I felt judged when Robbie challenged me about the laundry. I fell to my default of lying to cover up. This is *image management*. I will say or do something so others think better of me and accept me rather than reject me. Image management is nothing more than lying and lying starts in shame. Some may say that a lie about the amount of detergent in the bottom of the box is not a big deal. But it is. Lies, big or small, block intimacy in a marriage and therefore, the marriage suffers.

The Answer to Shame

Intimacy is not possible without risking rejection by telling the truth about yourself. This is completely counterintuitive. Everything in us yells to keep our shame secret, but God tells us to live a different way.

The answer to shame is confession. Confession simply means to agree with God. If God calls something a sin, confession is agreeing and calling what we have done a sin. 1 John 1:9 tells us "If we confess our sins, he is faithful and just and will forgive us our sins and purify us from all unrighteousness."

At some level, we are all willing to risk confessing to God. He already knows. Telling others is a different matter. The following verse is one of my favorites and I quote it often (as you may have noticed.) "Therefore confess your sins to each other and pray for each other so that you may be healed. The prayer of a righteous person is powerful and effective" (James 5:16). To be made whole and healed, we need to confess to God and others, especially our mates.

Robbie:

Confession, so we can have intimacy, has become a habit for John and me. Better than a date night, the honesty of showing each other our hearts and our weaknesses provide us with the moments of intimacy that make a marriage successful. (Don't get me wrong, date night is still very important.) If I see John across a room at a party and we lock eyes and smile, often it's because we know what each other are thinking. Why? Intimacy. Couples who have been married for a long period of time often finish each other's sentences. Why? Intimacy. The cost of being completely honest can be high but the benefits of intimacy are endless.

A writer named Sheldon Vanuaken wrote a book called *A Severe Mercy* that was published in 1977.[49] It is a deeply moving love story between Sheldon Van (Vanuaken) and his wife Davy and their slow conversion to Christianity (by way of letters to and from CS Lewis) before a tragedy befalls them. It is an excellent book. They were both very creative people who looked at life a little differently than most. In fact, they named seasons, moments, objects and even rhythms in their marriage. One rhythm they called the "Navigator's Council," was a set time to review where they'd been and where they were going.

I enjoyed *A Severe Mercy* and recently, I discovered a modern link that I just adore. I watch a few reality TV shows (don't judge me) and one of the ones I enjoy is *Little People, Big World* on The Learning Channel.[50] The oldest son got married a little over a year ago, and last week I watched an interview with him. Jeremy Roloff and his new wife Audrey have both read *A Severe Mercy* and love it. So they have incorporated a "Navigator's Council" into their own life.

The following is from Audrey Roloff's blog:

"Each week we ask each other a series of questions that we came to a consensus on during our honeymoon. Many of them are similar to the "marriage journal" questions that our premarital counselor's urged us to use, but we added/subtracted/changed a few. These are the seven questions we ask each other and record our answers in our Navigator's Council journal every Sunday.

1. What brought you joy this week?
2. What was something that was hard this week?
3. What's one specific thing I can do for you this week?
4. How can I pray for you this week?
5. Is there anything that's gone unsaid, convictions, confessions, unresolved hurt?
6. What's a dream, desire or thought that's been on the forefront of your mind this week?
7. Ask each other a question.

We always end our time in prayer, and once a month we ask two additional questions that we don't feel are necessary to ask each week.

1. How are we stewarding our finances?
2. How is our sex life?"[51]

The Roloffs, newlyweds in their early twenties, have got a handle on how to grow intimacy. After seeing this and talking about it, John and I have incorporated our own Iobst Council into our lives. Intimacy in your marriage is worth every bit of time and work.

Becoming one flesh is not just a physical act. It is a spiritual union. The man and wife are strands that God ties together. "A cord of three strands is not quickly broken" (Ecclesiastes 4:12). God, John, and I form a strong cord. Every time we lie or intentionally keep something from each other, we are fraying that cord. For the first seven years of our marriage, John and I did not practice confession at all, and we had no intimacy. We had sex, but no intimacy. Sex is very important in a marriage and is a beautiful gift God has given us. But true intimacy leads to great sex. Now, thanks be to God, we have true intimacy in our marriage which affects everything else in our relationship in a wonderfully positive way. It took that painful year of reconciliation for me to really allow John to "into me, see" and vice versa. I am so thankful we both made that choice.

Chapter Nineteen

Habit #4 – You Build Trust through Forgiveness

There is something so indescribably sweet and satisfying knowing that a husband or wife has forgiven the other freely, and from the heart.

—Henrik Ibsen[52]

John:

If you take our last recommendation to heart and seek increased intimacy in your marriage through confession, you might be faced with a new set of problems. After hearing a confession from your spouse, you need to forgive. The events and circumstances that will require your forgiveness may have violated your trust. Or you may be the one in need of forgiveness from your spouse and have lost his/her trust.

So the next step is to forgive and trust again—clearly simpler said than done. Let's start with what forgiveness is not and what forgiveness is and then we will move on to a simple (I didn't say easy, just simple) way to regain trust in your marriage.

What Forgiveness is Not:

- Forgiveness is not forgetting

The phrase "forgive and forget" is simply not true. God promises to cast our sins away. "He will again have compassion on us; you will tread our sins underfoot and hurl all our iniquities into the depths of the sea" (Micah 7:19). That sea is often referred to as the "sea of forgetfulness". We humans don't have access to that particular body of water.

We can choose not to harbor resentments over the past failures of others, but we will never truly forget.

- Forgiveness is not excusing the behavior.

I am convinced this is one of the great confusions in our society. Let me give you a simple example. If you are meeting someone for lunch and they arrive fifteen minutes late, they might say, "Please forgive me for being late; the traffic was a nightmare." They have asked for forgiveness and at the same time offered an excuse. So you have a dilemma: do you excuse them for being late since it was not their fault and out of their control? Or do you forgive them for the harm they caused because they were to blame, but you are releasing them? I believe this gets to the heart of what forgiveness is and what needs to happen for you to really forgive someone. And it is in stark contrast to excusing someone.

Excusing says:

You did not harm me. The harm I experienced was not your fault so you do not need to be accountable or forgiven.

Forgiveness says:

You did harm me. The harm I experienced was your fault so you do need to be held accountable or forgiven.

This may sound harsh but it is the heart of the matter. There is no need to forgive if there was no wrong. Confession is a statement from one person to another or God that says, "What I have done was wrong; I have no excuse and I am seeking forgiveness. And if possible, I am seeking a restoration of the broken parts of the relationship."

I am convinced that excusing damages the possibility of real forgiveness. So much so, that I recommend that when you are confessing a wrong that you say something to the effect of "I have no excuse" as part of the confession. Those words serve as a reminder to yourself (and the one you are asking to forgive you) that forgiveness is difficult and excusing is easy. Neither of you should settle for the easy way out.

Robbie:

The concept of forgiveness versus excusing is one we have learned to take seriously. So much so, that when I ask John or he asks me for forgiveness and either of us says, "No big deal" or "It's okay," the other interjects "No it was not okay. It was wrong and I need you to forgive me." If we just accept the "It's okay," then we've allowed them to excuse the behavior. And if someone excuses my behavior it communicates to me that if I do it again, it will again be *no big deal.*

In our society, forgiveness is going out of style accept for major offenses. This is not good. So we practice forgiveness, not excusing, in our home and we teach our son to do the same. When we hear from our teenager a phrase like "My bad" we stop him and teach him again the difference between excusing and forgiving.

John:

Forgiveness *Is*:

- Forgiveness is a long process (sometimes).

Forgiveness is not and does not have to be quick. There is a common church behavior where one person confesses and in the same breath asks "Will you forgive me?" and then stands there looking you in the eye expecting you will in that moment say, "Yes." You are, after all, a Christian and so you are somehow obligated to forgive immediately. Otherwise, it might be awkward and we can't have that. If the offense was as simple as being late for lunch, immediate forgiveness is probably appropriate, but if it is more complex or hurtful, it may take some time to process and you **should** take that time. Trying to rush will result in, at best, excusing and, at worst, an ongoing resentment because the forgiveness was not genuine. This resentment may leave you with feelings of guilt for not being a good enough Christian to simply forgive, which is a plot of the enemy of your heart.

Robbie:

- Forgiveness is Acknowledgement.

To forgive, it is vital to acknowledge that you have been wronged and that this person or group of people are responsible for that wrongdoing. Again, we sometimes feel that we need to sweep all offenses under a rug with the words "Being a Good Christian" crocheted on it. This is simply not true. Acknowledging that you were indeed hurt, and choosing to forgive whomever hurt you is healthy. If you were hurt and you say it was no big deal, you are allowing your own heart to be hurt again because you are not taking forgiveness seriously. Resentment could easily grow.

- Forgiveness is Taking Your Hands off Your Offender's Throat.

After acknowledging the truth of the offense, forgiveness is the act of making the conscious choice to take your hands off his/her throat and release them from any consequences, no matter how reasonable they may be. It may be consequences are appropriate and needed; you simply decide those consequences don't need to come from your hands. Instead, you give them to God who is a righteous judge and who alone can decide what consequences, if any, are needed.

John:

It is an absolute necessity to invite God into the process of forgiveness. Not simply because He has, through Christ, already forgiven you. But because you will need His healing hands on your heart and mind to forgive the kind of wounds that can come at the hands of someone as close and as trusted as a spouse. This is especially true where marriage vows about faithfulness have been violated. These are God-sized problems and require a God-sized solution. God can handle these problems and not only help us to forgive, but bring healing to the hurts on both sides.

To be clear, this part of forgiveness is between you and God and does not involve the offending party. This vertical aspect of forgiveness is essential. Without it, your forgiveness will be limited by your capacity for grace and will leave you with lingering resentment.

In some cases, where laws have been broken and abuse has occurred, it is still possible and vital to forgive and metaphorically remove your hands from your spouse's throat. As you begin the process of forgiveness, you can give your spouse to God and the police. Depending on the severity of the wrong, this will and should take time and may require the help of trusted friends, pastors and in some cases professional help from counselors.

Given the order of these holy habits, we are operating under the assumption that the required forgiveness is a result of confession. Sometimes however, you will be aware of an offence that was not confessed and the offending party has not repented and acknowledged their wrong. In these cases, this first phase still applies; take it to God and work out forgiveness between you and Him. The horizontal part of forgiveness that opens the door for relationship is not in place until the offending party is willing to confess the wrong. Suppose the wrong is from long ago and the offending party is no longer in your life. In that case, the process ends here because restoration of relationship and trust is not possible.

But when the offending party is your spouse asking for acknowledgement of the wrong, it is necessary for the horizontal phase of forgiveness to begin. It must be complete before you can start working towards the restoration of trust. It is also critically important that you forgive even if you don't feel like forgiving and even if the offending party hasn't acknowledged the wrong or asked for forgiveness. Failing to do so leaves you forever trapped as their victim.

Robbie:

I did not forgive John instantly. It was a very long process. At first, when I left him, I couldn't see ever forgiving him. In fact, I believed that separation and divorce was the solution. When I spent that first night at my friend Desha's house, God gave me the instruction to set my heart on pilgrimage. (Psalm 84:5) He didn't tell me to forgive and forget. I felt no compulsion to forgive him because I was a Christian. I felt angry and justified. God didn't come to me and tell me to feel differently. He simply told me to not give up. By setting my heart on pilgrimage, I was giving God control, even as I was furious. Forgiveness came later, little by little, as God worked on both of our hearts.

I was tempted to "excuse" John many times. I mean, men are men, right? Pornography and masturbation are just part of life, right? He is not really hurting me through any of this. For me to forgive John I faced up to the real harm his addiction did to our marriage and to my heart. I looked at John's behavior and acknowledged it was wrong and hurtful and caused damage.

John:

One more thing that forgiveness is Not:

Forgiveness is Not the Same as Trust

Regaining trust is a complex problem with a simple solution, but it must be proceeded by forgiveness. Trying to trust your spouse before you have forgiven him/her leads to excusing their behavior, in effect, saying it was no big deal. Excusing does not lead to trust in marriage; it creates hidden resentment. Take the time you need to get with God so He can help you forgive your spouse and start the healing process of your heart, the restoration of your relationship and the possibility to true intimacy based on the truth.

Restoring trust is as simple as this:
Consistent Behavior over Time.

The one who has done the wrong needs to change and be consistent about that change for a long enough period of time so that trust can be restored. The one who was harmed needs enough time to trust again.

Now for some important ground rules:

- The person who violated the trust gets no say about how much time is needed. In fact, as a general rule every time they whine or complain about how long it is taking, the trust time "shot clock" resets to zero.
- The person who has had their trust violated gets no say about what consistent behavior is or should be.

Let's go back to our story for examples of this. In our case, I was the one who violated trust so I alone was responsible for consistent behavior. Examples of this for me were:

- Committing to recovery and sobriety.
- Relapse and setbacks are a normal part of recovery so consistent behavior doesn't mean perfection, but it does mean a serious commitment.
- Regular attendance at recovery meetings and counseling sessions.

- Significant increase in accountability to Robbie for my time.
- Lying was a regular part of my addiction so I needed to let Robbie know where I was and what I was doing and if anything changed to let her know immediately.
- Be honest about my thoughts, feelings and actions including full disclosure about my past lies and behaviors, especially my acting out. (Furniture Moving Days)

And as I mentioned earlier, no whining about how long it would take for Robbie to trust me again. That was none of my business.

Robbie:

In being responsible for the time, I had to first and foremost commit my heart to being patient and waiting. Consistent behavior was vital for me to stay in our marriage. But recovery takes time and although I was in charge of deciding **when** I would trust John, I made the decision to give our marriage a year to heal. I committed to staying and working for healing.

Any man might try to control the time with remarks like "Are you ever going to trust me?" and "I haven't looked at pornography for a month – what is it going to take?" But John was not in charge of time, so when I decided to begin trusting him was completely up to me.

In the same way, I was not in charge of his consistency, but I wanted to be. I became a private investigator and decided it was my responsibility to make sure John was being consistent. I did this by checking his computer, looking through receipts and demanding that he go to meetings and counseling sessions.

Becoming a private investigator does not work.

In the course of building trust, asking questions like "Where were you?" or "Have you acted out today?" are absolutely fine. Honest answers are needed to build trust. However, asking questions and trying to control my husband's behavior are two different things.

If John came home late, it would be fine for me to ask "Where were you?" and "Are you still sober?" However, it would not be fine and actually futile to go through his wallet or demand that he go to a meeting that night. This is very difficult for any woman who has been betrayed. But trying to control John's behavior never worked.

For example, I went to the computer once and found a file on it labeled "Conjoined." I did not trust John at all yet. A couple of nights previous to this, there was a story on the news about conjoined twin women. When you are full of anger and distrust, it is quite simple to conclude that your spouse is cheating or lying in some way no matter what. So my first thought was the file was full of nude pictures of conjoined twins. (Looking back, this is a bit humorous to me, but at the time it was not.)

I was learning about how to build trust in counseling, so I knew that I didn't want to open the file. First, I didn't want to see those pictures and second, it would be private investigator behavior. So I decided to talk to John about it. I remember feeling so angry that he was back at it. It was vital to be able to talk about what I was feeling and thinking.

"John, I found something on the computer."

"What?"

"A file." I am sure my tone was part fury, part seething.

"Okay?"

I told him my thoughts and suspicions.

"It's not porn, Robbie."

"Show me."

John went with me to the computer and opened the file. Sure enough, it was an assignment from his night school. I did my part, bringing up what I needed without trying to control him and he did his part – consistent behavior.

John:

Since my wrongs were sexual in nature, a natural and reasonable consequence was a period of abstinence until trust was restored. Since this was new territory for us we sought the advice of trusted friends, sponsors and counselors before becoming sexual again. In our case, we were celibate for eight months and then renewed our marriage vows with friends on a beach in San Diego before having a second "wedding night". The waiting was difficult but it was worth it for us both. If you try to hurry and avoid the natural and reasonable consequences to the harm you caused, you will lose in the long run.

Robbie:

Choosing celibacy was a wonderful decision because when we renewed our vows and had sex, we did it on a foundation of trust. Trust was not fully developed between us at that time, but enough trust existed that I felt very comfortable being intimate. It took years for me to fully trust John. His consistent behavior made the time go quicker.

John:

One of the challenges with forgiveness in marriage is the idea that *if they loved me they would never do that.* Clearly this is an issue where the offense is sexual in nature, but to some degree it applies regardless of the wrong. I believe this is related to the expectations we bring into marriage, some reasonable and some ridiculous.

Expectations like:

- Since I'm a good person I could only love a good person and good people don't hurt the ones they love.
- If they love me I won't need to tell them how I feel; they'll just know.

- All my needs are normal and reasonable and should be met by my spouse.
- "Love means never having to say you're sorry." (Yes, I quoted the movie.)[53]

We all enter marriage with expectations and when our spouse confesses a wrong, some of those expectations will be called into question. If your spouse can't meet your expectations, then it is easy to go to a place where you assume that your spouse doesn't really love you or is not on your side. When you start to believe that, hopelessness about the marriage quickly follows and divorce starts to feel like a reasonable option. We all know that God hates divorce, but He doesn't want me to be treated like this, and surely He has someone out there who would love me in the right way, right?

This kind of thinking makes doing the work to forgive and regain trust seem unreasonable. Many marriages end in divorce because of this kind of thinking, even among committed Christians.

If you are in a place right now where divorce is appealing, please put that thought on hold for at least a year and instead do the work of forgiveness. See if God can't do for you what He did for us. God can bring the joy of a marriage that works back into your life.

3rd Overarching Principle

Your Spouse is a Unique Gift from God, not Your Enemy

When I realize that God makes his gifts fit each person, there's no way I can covet what you got because it just wouldn't fit me.
—William P. Smith[54]

Chapter Twenty

Habit #5 – Honor Your Spouse with Your Words

The tongue has no bones but is strong enough to break a heart.
—Anonymous[55]

Robbie:

Early in our marriage, on a summer night in San Diego, John and I invited two couples over for dinner. We were part of a "couples-dinner-6," a group that met once a month for a meal. We took turns hosting and this month Cheryl and Jack, Theresa and Jeff would be coming over. We'd been married just a little over two years and I was very excited to impress our married couple friends with how wonderful we were doing. Plus, I made a new potato dish that was going to be fabulous.

I have to confess that in our first years of marriage I was extremely high strung. (John would laugh at this understatement.) My public versus private philosophy guided my every move, so making sure that our guests thought I was an incredible wife made the top of my priority list. So much so that my nerves were frayed. When we were about to serve the meal, I took the potato dish out of the oven and promptly dropped it. The glass dish shattered and scrumptious potato fixings became crunchy shards scattered over the kitchen floor. I was mortified. As John helped me clean, I called my apologies to our guests. My skin burned and I wanted to just die. Our friends were extremely kind about it and we settled down to a good meal, minus any fabulous potatoes.

In this atmosphere, John and I once again played our go-to roles when we were with other people. Both of us are naturally quick-witted and we each enjoy making others laugh. It was easy for us to shoot zingers toward each other and the sharp-pointed words always ended in laughter. On this night, the subject of money came up. I have never been very good with money and John knew this. So he got ready, aimed and fired, making jokes about my lack of money skills. We all laughed. I followed later by making fun of the lack of John's spelling skills. Again, laughter. We both laughed along with everyone else.

After our guests left, I silently stewed like a pot of soup on the way to a hard boil. With my passive aggressive silent treatment, perfected by this time in our marriage, I made him know I was upset.

"Are you okay?" John asked.

"I'm fine." *Of course you know I am not okay, you jerk!*

"Robbie, what's wrong?"

I blew up at my husband and told him to never talk to me that way again in front of guests. (Notice I didn't tell him to not talk to me like that ever, but in front of guests. Further evidence of my "everything is about appearances" attitude.) How dare he make me feel so small after I already felt embarrassed and stupid about the disastrous potato dish? John apologized and we went to bed. It never happened again.

Until we were in public with each other the next time.

John:

Robbie and I are both intelligent people with a gift for words. We each have a finely tuned wit I like to call the spiritual gift of sarcasm. But in our early marriage, we used our gifts of language and humor as a weapon to harm each other. It was going to require a change of heart for us to begin to use our gifts for good.

"With the tongue we praise our Lord and Father, and with it we curse human beings who have been made in God's likeness" (James 3:9).

The words we choose, the tone we give them and the impact they have is largely a choice and reflection of the intent of my heart.

"A good man brings good things out of the good stored up in his heart, and an evil man brings evil things out of the evil stored up in his heart. For the mouth speaks what the heart is full of" (Luke 6:45).

If asked, Robbie and I would each say we loved the other and wanted the best for each other. But the cutting words we used told a different and truer story. We each wanted our own way and we each sought to use humor to get attention, even at the expense of our spouse.

In the middle of our year of reconciliation, we consciously made a choice.

We committed to honoring one another with our words.

Robbie:

We would get in the car, headed out to church or a party. A place where we would be with friends. One of us would say, "I will honor you with my words tonight."

The other would respond in like.

When we began this practice, we didn't have wonderful feelings toward each other. I was still angry and John was still living in shame. To say this to each other was a complete act of our wills as if we were taking medicine that we couldn't feel, but believed would help our sick marriage.

At times, we'd forget and a sharpened knife of humor would fly across the room landing in our beloved's heart. But being conscious of our promise made us apologize quickly. Over and over we would say "I will honor you with my words." And God honored this and used our words to start building each other up.

One of the first times John really bragged on me in public during this year surprised me. My first thought was that he wanted something and that his words were an insincere attempt at manipulation. But over time I began to believe him and appreciate his encouragement. I tried to return the favor. In the past I spoke well of him in public so that others would see us as a Godly couple. Now I spoke well of him because I chose to see the true good in him. What other people thought was no longer the point.

By the next year (it took a while) using our words to love and encourage each other became a habit. Soon we didn't need to make the promise in our car on the way to a party. We just did it naturally.

Since my love language is words of affirmation, this change in our communication had a profound effect on my heart. I discovered that John was indeed, for me. Knowing that my partner in life was in my corner made for a huge leap in the healing of our marriage.

John:

Honoring your spouse with your words is much more than the advice from mom that says "if you don't have something nice to say, don't say anything." It is much more like what Jesus said to the Pharisees in Matthew 12:34, "For out of the overflow of the heart the mouth speaks."

Honoring is a choice to support intimacy as we defined it earlier - "Tell the truth about your thoughts, feeling and actions." We choose to do that in a way that honors the dignity of the other. It becomes much more than being polite or even kind. It is a decision to cherish our mate.

This type of communication will have the most powerful effect in your marriage if you practice it in three separate spheres of communication:

Honor your Spouse with your Words when you are Together with No One Else Around

In some ways this was the most difficult, because this is where we gave ourselves permission to be truly mean-spirited and hurtful with each other. We each engaged in a form of image management or Robbie's philosophy of public vs. private. We could be downright vicious with each other and keep the illusion of being the perfect couple as long as we only did it when no one was around to hear it.

Honoring with our words when we are alone means that we must be kind and edit our first thoughts, especially in an argument. Couples know the buttons to push to hurt their loved ones' hearts. When we are alone and communicating, we avoid those buttons. If it is a discussion where sensitive subjects must be addressed, then we take time to use compassion and diplomacy.

Honor your Spouse with your Words when Others Are Present

Robbie and I redefined how humor should be used. Taking cheap shots at each other for a laugh was the easiest way to enjoy a night with friends. Honoring each other with our words was a way of reminding ourselves that we committed to hold the other's heart as a precious and valued thing that we should esteem.

With practice, we found that we can still laugh and enjoy our nights out without putting a target on each other. Now, when we see couples who put each other down in public over and over, we know that something is going on in their marriage God needs to address. Teasing your mate is one thing and it's something we all do. But attacking is different. As a couple, you should each know where you draw the line between the two.

Honor your Spouse with your Words when they are not Present

This too, was a difficult habit to change. Even in Christian circles I have noticed a tendency for men to speak about their wives in a way that would get them hit in the head with a blender if their wives were present. Worst of all, this disrespectful communication often comes in the form of a prayer request. "Please pray for my wife's horrible habit of nagging me." To consciously honor Robbie when she was not present required more than curbing my wit, but also fighting against the stream of "acceptable" behavior, or in other words, complaining about my wife.

Robbie:

Let me inject here that dishonoring your husband when he is not there is extremely common in circles of women. It's not just man-bashing, it is husband-bashing. To "vent" about the annoying or horrible things my husband does is unfortunately acceptable among Christians. Please understand that I know it is important for us women to talk about our problems. But I have discovered if I need to vent about John, I have two women I talk to. Two. Not my entire Bible study or even at a small lunch. If I make a habit of speaking dishonorably about John, something happens in me. As the negative words tumble out of my mouth, my heart is reinforced with negativity towards him. We can be honest about our problems with our husbands without throwing them under a bus in front of a bunch of our women-friends. I've also seen and felt the temptation to do this when several other women are doing it. If I am at lunch with some gals and husband-bashing begins, it is easy to jump into the conversation, just so I can be a part of the action. To change this behavior requires a conscious decision which results in a marriage that is sweeter, simply because we don't bash our men behind their backs.

John:

In the years that have followed, my heart has changed. By speaking to and about Robbie with words that convey that she is my friend, lover, confidant and a great gift from our King Jesus, I truly see her that way.

There is a saying in addiction recovery, "Take the actions and the feelings will follow".

When we decided to honor one another with our words, I must admit that I didn't feel like it. But taking the actions and developing the habit has made room in my heart for those very feelings. We no longer stop and agree to honor each other before going into every public setting. Not because we have changed our minds but because to do otherwise would today be as ridiculous as stabbing myself in the chest with a knife. Robbie's heart is a cherished thing to me and I would no more harm her than I would harm myself.

Honor your Spouse with your Words by NOT Comparing

Robbie:

Comparison is dangerous in a marriage and can be quite destructive.

I have had problems with comparing for most of my life. I believe my insecurity bred comparison. When I left John, I compared my poor lot in life to everyone else who looked as if they were happy. It only led to self-pity. When I have compared John to other men, the Spirit has convicted me and whispered that in comparing I am subtly saying that John is not my unique and wonderful gift from God. When I have compared my marriage to others, the enemy attacks me with insecurity and jealousy. When I compare my responsibilities with John it often leads to silly fights about who does more housework or who spends more time with Noah. Marriage is not fair. It is futile to think otherwise.

Theodore Roosevelt said, "Comparison is the thief of joy."[56]

Choosing to honor John by not comparing is allowing joy to reign in our marriage.

John:

For Robbie and me the primary issue that required forgiveness and the rebuilding of trust was my sexual acting out. As a result, it was intuitive for me to compare myself to what I assumed other husbands did. As a result, I lived under the shadow of being the "bad guy" and the cause of all of our issues and problems.

That is a place that can lead to even more shame and shame inevitably leads back to the addiction.

An even more dangerous attitude would be for me to compare sins and hurts and in my judgement conclude that Robbie's harm to me was worse that my harm to her. This kind of judgement leads to self-righteousness and justification of my "lesser sins" and again, I'm back to the addiction. Additionally, from that place I feel justified in withholding forgiveness and trust until "that woman" makes it right.

Robbie:

I was the queen of comparing sins in our marriage. My sins were nothing compared to John's sins. What a lie that is. The more I reinforced this lie in our home, the more dishonorable my treatment of my husband.

John:

As you can see comparison, regardless of whether I come out on top or bottom, is dangerous and will make the possibility of forgiveness and trust impossible and will likely lead back to addictive behavior.

I am convinced this is because of the evil twins of pride and shame. In any form of comparison, I tend to find myself better than or worse than. When I judge myself better it is pride and when I judge myself worse than, it is shame.

Men seem to have this uncontrollable need to compare themselves to other men. If I walk into a room with fifty other men who I don't know I almost automatically create a "pecking order" based on some random criteria without really knowing anything about them. I will quickly sort them into two groups. Those who are above me and those who are below me. I will then feel some sense of pride and shame for where I am in the group. Notice that I don't split the fifty into three groups—over me, under me and like me. In my sinful judgement I am always special and unique and never "just another Bozo on the bus".

The major problem here is that I have now allowed pride and shame to tell me who I am, rather than believing what God has said about my identity. That is why I am convinced that any form of comparison is sin. For me to believe anything that disagrees with God's assessment of me is to call God a liar.

We need to instead take Paul's example when he referred to himself as the worst of sinners and the least of the apostles. (1 Timothy 1:16) Paul is not struggling with low self-image or shame. He is coming from a place of humility. The idea isn't to make comparisons and judgements and simply always lose. The idea is to have the humility to not judge or compare myself to another, especially my spouse. The way I hold Paul's idea of being the worst of sinners and least of apostles is to hold onto the idea that when it comes to Robbie and me, I'm the lucky one. I married up.

I can never repay for the harm that I caused and never be sufficiently grateful for the grace and forgiveness she has extended to me. I need never feel less than or once again put on the cloak of shame. I am a fully loved, forgiven and redeemed son of God. And it is from that knowledge that I am free to have the humility to love and appreciate Robbie and the gift she is to me.

Robbie:

Humility is the answer for me, too. I am so blessed to have John and I am no better or worse than he. We are both saved by grace and doing the best we can. Honoring each other with our words reinforces that truth.

Chapter Twenty-One

Habit #6 – Accept Responsibility and Fight Fair.

If two people who love each other let a single instant wedge itself between them, it grows—it becomes a month, a year, a century; it becomes too late.

—Jean Giraudoux [57]

John:

I was raised by my mom and aunt, two single women who did the best they could in raising a boy dedicated to secrecy by the age of eight. As I grew up, one of the lessons I learned was that conflict was the unpardonable sin. Therefore, I never caused conflict. I never engaged in conflict. This didn't mean I always agreed with what was going on. It just meant that I would never voice my disagreement. This led to a condition where I was always *NICE*. Nice is a four letter word and I have come to categorize it with those other four letter words we don't use in church. Being "nice" meant I should lie and withhold my heart by never expressing my opinion if I didn't fully agree. Please recall that my operating definition of intimacy is to tell the truth about my thoughts, feelings and behavior. When I refused to have conflict and instead remained "nice" I was, by that definition, incapable of being intimate. This served my sex addiction very well because sex addiction is, at its core, an intimacy disorder.

So I entered our marriage with no skills at successful conflict, only being "nice" and avoidance.

Robbie:

I was raised by a wonderful married couple who dearly loved each other. However, my siblings and I never witnessed them fight. Ever. I am sure they disagreed but I can't remember that happening in front of us either.

My father was a great dad, but his temper could easily flare out of control. He would spew profanity but never hit us. My mother, although a strong independent woman, would react in silence when Daddy went off. I remember Mama looking at me with a signal to be quiet and to stay out of Daddy's way. I developed a fear of his rage.

As I reached adulthood, this anxiety became terror of anyone's anger. So when I was in a situation where someone became angry due to conflict, my fear would flare up and I would try to disappear into silence or quickly make peace.

So I entered our marriage with no skills at conflict, only a huge fear of anger and a desperation for peace at all times.

John:

During the first years of our marriage we avoided having any conflict with each other at any cost. We talked about nothing difficult, just swept it under the carpet. I did this to be "nice" and Robbie did this to avoid any emotional anger.

As we neared the breaking point when Robbie left me, we began to fight. In our short quarrels, I would throw off the "nice" act and say something harsh to Robbie and immediately leave the room. It was my best move – get the last mean word in and run away.

Robbie:

The way I engaged in our fights was two-fold. First, I was scared to death that John would yell at me. (Although in 20 years, he has never yelled at me.) And for some reason, I equated that anger with John leaving. My dad never left my mom or vice versa, so I think this fear was just a reflection of my deep insecurity at the time. So if we argued, my immediate response was terror.

Second, I felt that as a Christian we should never let the sun go down on our anger – that's Biblical right? So I interpreted that as a need for immediate resolution to any conflict. We must have peace at all times. So when we did fight and John would shoot his last bullet at me and leave the room, I would follow him, now terrified that if we didn't resolve this, we would leave each other and also disappoint Jesus. So I doggedly chased him so we could be good Christians.

John:

Having Robbie follow me around the house, begging for us to "talk it out" only infuriated me more. Knowing that Robbie feared any escalation of an argument, I would just look like I was about to become aggressive or loud. Usually she backed off.

We had no clue how to fight fair.

Learning good conflict skills was like learning to honor one another with our words. It started as a decision and over time became a feeling. We can disagree about an idea, thing or behavior without attacking the person or their heart to make our point.

I had to learn how to not be "nice." This meant I learned to tell the truth about how I was feeling, even if it would mean an argument.

Robbie:

First, I had to deal with my fear of anger. This took some counseling and really working out why loud emotions scared me. With John, I had to learn to live with unresolved conflict. Sometimes John just needs time to process. Trying to force peace and agreement is a futile process without allowing time for my husband to think.

We are still not stellar at conflict resolution, but we are getting better all the time. Part of improving our communication in arguments is leaning on experts in fighting fair. The following information comes from a barrage of marriage conferences and a wonderful class our pastor, Anthony Pranno, taught about conflict in a marriage.

Unhealthy Responses

If you or your spouse are having a disagreement, these four responses are neither helpful or healthy.

1. **Avoiding.** John and I are both great at this. He was great at leaving in a huff and I knew how to emotionally shut down.
2. **Defensiveness.** When faced with a conflict, it is the art of defensiveness to turn the tables. John and I both knew how to make whatever we were confronted with not about the issue at hand, but about the other person's character. It's sneaky but effective. And incredibly unhealthy.
3. **Invalidation.** Another tactic to make your spouse be the bad guy is to tear into their character and attack with "You're crazy" or "You're overreacting." Instead of dealing with the problem head on, invalidation tries to veer the argument to a discussion about your spouse's weaknesses or faults.
4. **Intensification.** This is the explosion, the yelling and the slamming of doors which is all about emotion and not about resolution.

Fighting Fair Principles

The following principles for fighting fair have helped us a great deal:

1. **Don't just walk out of an argument.** Leaving without saying anything is hurtful and piles on the anger so it becomes a mound of animosity. If you need to leave an argument to calm down or process what happened, have the courtesy to tell your mate why you are leaving.

2. **The words "never" and "always" should be avoided.** They never help resolve conflict, but always make it worse. (See what I did there?) If you are disagreeing and you tell your spouse "You always" or "You never" it is a direct attack on their character. When you have conflict, your aim should be to resolve it, not to draw blood.

3. **When you or your spouse are angry, it is better to schedule a time to talk about the disagreement and not address it when emotions are running high.** Emotions cloud resolution. I learned to let John have his time to process before talking about our differences. While he was calming down, I had a chance to think clearly about the disagreement and not only through the eyes of "We *must* resolve this quickly." I also learned to live with unresolved issues for a while. My desperation to have peace came out of insecurity. That insecurity blocked valid resolution as much as anger.

4. **Shut up and listen.** The two most powerful words you can say in an argument are "Go On." It communicates to your mate that you want to hear their side of the argument. You want to understand. Many couples argue with the sole purpose of winning, not understanding their partner or even being

understood themselves. Make a conscious effort to *listen* more than talk during a conflict.

5. **Negotiate and Compromise.** If you want to get your way all the time, you shouldn't be married. Compromise is the oil of the engine of marriage. It is important to be willing to give in a little so a conflict can be resolved.

6. **It is more important to love your spouse than to be right.** This statement smacks at the pride that each of us possess. Being right is a way to feel good about myself, so the more I am right, the better I feel. If you place this philosophy into marriage, you will find your marriage is miserable. Sometimes, as in parenting, we have to choose our battles. I know that I am right most of the time, but I give in often, because it is more important to me to have a good marriage based on love, not winning arguments. (John would disagree and say that he is right most of the time. Since we each have cornered the market on being right, it is a mystery to us how our marriage ever went so wrong.) Bottom line – loving is more important than winning.

Robbie:

Communication and conflict resolution are vital to a happy marriage. But both are difficult unless you practice them with your spouse. The word "practice" should be your intention. No one is perfect at this, but the Spirit of God can always help. I love what Paul wrote in Philippians 4:9, "Whatever you have learned or received or heard from me, or seen in me—put it into practice. And the God of peace will be with you." Practice healthy conflict resolution. Pray about your conflicts. Pray individually and together. Invite God into your fights. If you have children, arguing in front of them with no rancor or malice is a wonderful teaching tool for their future relationships.

John:

It is not possible for two different people to share a life together without conflict. Having conflict in your marriage doesn't mean that you don't love one another or that your marriage is bad; it is simply an opportunity to grow in oneness and intimacy and put your own selfish desires aside.

Robbie:

He thought he got in the last word.

4th Overarching Principle

It's Time to Let Go of your Wedding-Day Expectations and be Married to your Actual Spouse.

When you stop expecting people to be perfect, you can like them for who they are.
—Donald Miller[58]

Chapter Twenty-two

Habit #7 – Break the Need for Control.

You must do the thing you think you cannot do.
—Eleanor Roosevelt[59]

Robbie:

If a woman has a uterus, or has ever had a uterus, she is a control freak. I believe this with all my…uterus. I've talked to many, many women whose life goal is to control their husbands, children, siblings, friends and co-workers. It was part of the curse that God established with Eve. God told her that the second part of her punishment for sin was "your desire will be for your husband, and he will rule over you" (Genesis 3:16). We always want control.

When I married John, I was willing to ignore the red flags I encountered because I wanted to get married and have someone love me. I was desperate and in my desperation I didn't think. So when John told me he was a sex addict and that he was better, I let it slide on by. However, I also assumed that when we were married he would have no problems, he would be a wonderful spiritual leader and he would court me every day. Why? Because I would "teach" him. I would be his "helpmate."

I would control him.

Soon after we were married I found my first area that I needed to control: the public persona of our marriage. I knew something was wrong. I found evidence of his addiction occasionally. However, I controlled our image by telling everyone what a Godly man John was and how our marriage was pretty wonderful.

During our reconciliation, I tried desperately to control his spirituality. His Christianity needed to look like mine in order to work, right? So many of us women crave a man to be a spiritual leader, but we will not let go of control so God can get a hold of his heart.

Finally, I wanted to control who he is. I fell in love with his humor, but after I'd been married to it for a while, I wanted his humor to be different. I wanted to control when he was funny and how he was funny.

In order for our marriage to be healed, I had to take a daring leap off of Mount I-am-In-Charge and allow God to be in control, not me. It was one of the most difficult steps I've ever taken.

John:

"Men marry women with the hope they will never change. Women marry men with the hope they will change. Invariably they are both disappointed."—Albert Einstein.[60]

During our year of reconciliation, I discovered Einstein was right. I imagine that Robbie was just as frustrated that I wasn't changing as I was frustrated that she seemed to have changed.

I was now on a mission to make her into the woman she was before we married. Essentially back to the woman who wasn't concerned about trying to change me, as she was before our wedding. The woman who married me and kept my secret.

I did this is by trying to control her in two primary ways. First, I resisted her efforts to change me. My usual argument was that it was not reasonable for her to expect that I feel the same way she felt to the same degree. Or I would try to make her feel bad about any expectations she brought into the marriage by labeling them as unreasonable. Second, I would encourage thoughts and attitudes like before we were married, often turning to shaming behavior. For example, Robbie would let me know something about herself that I didn't know before we married. I would usually "joke" that I should have required a "full disclosure" before our wedding. That sarcastic comment carried the message that I might not have married her if I knew "that" about her. In short, my efforts to be in control and in charge had me behaving like a total jerk and left Robbie beaten and wounded.

Even if you get your way and succeed at controlling your wife, you will still lose. Your bride is God's gift to you. Even the aspects of her you wish you could change are part of that gift. Controlling her to suit your desires is the same as telling God that He gives bad gifts.

The Law of Unintended Consequence

Actions and decisions have consequences—cause and effect. I turn the steering wheel and the car turns. This is what is known as an intended consequence. But if the roads are icy, steering can result in an out of control slide. That is *an unintended consequence*.

The intended consequence of control in a marriage is to change your spouse into the version you feel you deserve. You may even tell yourself that if they change they will become the version of themselves that God intended in the first place.

The unintended consequences include:

Dissatisfaction. When you focus on your spouse as someone who needs to be changed, you can't help but feel dissatisfied with your spouse as they are. As a result of those feelings, you can't help but act like you are not satisfied and come off as a disapproving parent.

Mistrust. The unintended consequence of dissatisfaction and disapproval is the feeling that your spouse if against you. He/she no longer seeks your good or blessing and instead, only wants to harm you.

The problem with control it that it is based on judgement. And even worse, the assumption that your judgement about what is right and wrong is the only correct judgement. It doesn't matter that your spouse has their own judgement and it is different than yours. If they disagree, they must be wrong.

Remember back when you fell in love and decided to get married? You were *for* each other and you were certain that your spouse was *for you*. You were each other's biggest cheerleaders. The act of control undermines that sense of security and safety in the relationship.

The Letting Go of Control Clap

Robbie:

We have learned a "trick" that has helped us with our desire to control the other. In fact, it has saved us many times. It might help save your marriage, too.

If you have ever been to a casino and played black jack, you know that when a dealer leaves and a new dealer comes to the table, a ritual takes place. The dealer who is leaving rubs his/her hands together and then opens them to show the players (and the video camera and the mafia men who are watching) that they are leaving the table with nothing in their hands and they are giving up control of the game.

Somehow, and I don't know exactly how, John and I turned this action into clapping and then showing our spouse our empty hands. Try it. Clap twice and show your hands to your partner. Feels good, right?

This is John's and my way of saying "I am not in control of you" or "I wouldn't have done it that way." We have learned to apply this in significant and insignificant situations and it has saved us from many arguments.

For example, John might say to me, "Robbie can I clean the kitchen for you?"

And I say, "Of course, beloved." (I don't actually use the term 'beloved.')

He will clean it for me. However, when I walk into said kitchen, I notice something. (Women, I bet you know what I am going to write here.) The counters are not clean. Cleaning the kitchen to John does not include wiping down the counters.

So I say, "Beloved?"

Now at this moment I have a choice. I can make a big deal out of it, which I have, or I can clap my hands twice and say, *Oh well. I wouldn't have done it that way. But I am not John and I cannot control him.*

You see, if I want it done a certain way I need to communicate instructions to John or I need to let go of control of the situation. And this is not just a wife to husband scenario.

I hate to put gas in the car. I feel those moments of sticking the thingy into the gas hole and hitting the numbered gas button and then pulling the trigger is a waste of my life. I do not like it. So, in our marriage, John has taken on the job of putting gas in our cars. However, sometimes I am out and about and I notice the gas gauge is at empty. I have to put some gas in. So I do and I go home and say, "Beloved? (I don't really say beloved) The car needs gas. I put some in to get home."

John will ask, "How much did you put in?"

I answer, "A dollar."

Now at this moment, John has a choice to make. Either he can make a big deal out of it, and he has, or he can clap his hands and say, *Oh well. I wouldn't have done it that way. But I am not Robbie and I cannot control her.*

See how wonderfully it works? It has saved us countless arguments. Simply by practicing the act of letting go. The same principle applies in more significant areas. I discovered it was impossible to control John's spirituality. His relationship with God is his relationship, not mine, and he must be in control of it. Not me. If I do try to control him, it ends in frustration and arguments.

Common Areas of Control

Many women I have talked to have the same complaint in their marriage: "I wish my husband was our family's spiritual leader." Most of the time, the women who complain about this, try to control the way their husbands lead their family. It is one thing to say "Honey, you lead us." It is another to say "Honey, you lead us. But you better do these three things because that's what I would do."

If you want your husband to be your family's spiritual leader, get out of God's way and let God deal with your husband. Instead of talking, pray. Pray a lot. And watch what God does.

When we ask our husbands to be the spiritual leader, we need to be willing to let them lead in the way that God tells them. Clap, clap!

Early in our marriage I wanted John to plan our date nights. However, when he did, I would be disappointed and change his plans. John quickly decided that he didn't want to plan our dates. I mean, why do it when he knows he will disappoint me? The expectations we put on our husbands can beat them down to a point they do nothing, simply because they don't want to fail. Again.

So when John plans a date night for us, I go into the night with an attitude of gratitude. I thank him for what he planned and I choose to enjoy it, even if it is not what I would have planned. Clap, clap!

John:

Like virtually every couple, we didn't come to our marriage with the same attitude about money. I am more likely to say no to unplanned expenses and Robbie is more likely to say yes. I would frame the conversations from the perspective that my approach was right and the only approach that honored God. As a result, every conversation about money had me being right and often the "parent" and Robbie feeling wrong or guilty. We got to the point that every time Robbie needed to talk about money with me, it would start with her being guilty and apologetic. I would take advantage of that by being a jerk about anything she ever asked for.

Now to be fair, my methods with money had its flaws. My approach was formed by a basic mistrust of never having enough, so I have struggled with giving to God and others. Robbie, on the other hand, is the most naturally generous person I have ever met. Additionally, when Robbie would deviate from the "budget" it would tend to be in amounts of 10 to 20 dollars. But I would deviate from the "budget" by buying a race car or a motorcycle or flying lessons. So Robbie would deviate a few times a week and I would "only" deviate a few times a decade but if you add it up I spent more than she did.

I now know trying to control Robbie is futile. We have discussions about money and we still look at it completely differently. But we live on a budget with no secrets. It is not my job to control Robbie's spending habits and shame her when she goes over the budget. It is my job to discuss our expectations with her and pray for her to live within our means. Clap! Clap!

Robbie:

An added note: it is common for women to try to control men with nagging or withholding sex. Both are wrong and against God's best for our marriage.

John:

Men try to control women with silence and emotional unavailability. Neither honor our wives or our God and His plan for marriage.

Letting go of Control—Examples from *The Serenity Prayer*

John:

The Serenity Prayer is popular among the recovery community and teaches lessons about life and particularly control.

> *God grant me the serenity to accept the things I cannot change, the courage to change the things I can, and the wisdom to know the difference.*
> ### —Reinhold Niebuhr [61]

The prayer is basically requesting three attributes: serenity, courage and wisdom. Each are connected to the matter of control.

We humans naturally seek to control situations and people. The reason this prayer is a mainstay in twelve step meetings is that addicts take that desire to control to unhealthy extremes and need supernatural intervention to deal with an out of balance approach to life.

Let's look at each part of the prayer.

God Grant me the Serenity to
Accept the Things I Cannot Change

When faced with things we cannot change (or control) we are left frustrated and resentful. This part of the prayer is a plea for supernatural intervention in the form of God-given serenity in the face of those unsettling emotions when life just won't go the way I think it ought to go.

Mark Owen, one of the Navy Seals from Team 6 wrote in his book *No Hero* about a lesson he learned during a rock climbing trip. He froze in fear 300 feet up and found himself paralyzed so he couldn't go any further. His instructor made his way over to him and told him to "Stay in your three-foot world." When Mark asked what he was talking about the instructor said, "Look, you can't affect anything outside of three feet around you so stay in your three-foot world. Look inside that three-foot world, find the next hand hold and climb your way out." Mark did and has since lived that philosophy.[62]

The "three-foot world" is a great example of accepting things I cannot change. We try to control people and circumstances that are beyond our reach. Additionally, if it has a will of its own, it's probably out of my control. As a starting point, if it's not "me" it is probably out of my control. Since so much of the universe is outside of me, including my spouse, I am going to need a great deal of acceptance and serenity to get through my day.

The Courage to Change the Things I Can

Using the same guidelines as above, the things I can and should change are generally limited to little more than me. Given the human tendency towards control and our use of that control to make others behave in a way that pleases us, we have a glaring tendency to assume we are right and in no need of changing at all. The whole problem with the world or my spouse is that they won't do it my way. This is especially true in marriage.

Given that assumption we are very well practiced in trying to change everything but ourselves. Recovery calls for us to change first by realizing that we need to change and then by seeking divine intervention in the form of the courage to change.

The Wisdom to Know the Difference

The serenity to change the things I can refers to attitudes, situations or people that are not mine to change. *The courage to change the things I can* refers to the attitudes, situations and actions that are mine to change. *The wisdom to know the difference* is asking God to help me know if something is mine to deal with or not mine and I should just let it go. In those cases, this last part of the prayer is an admission that we lack the wisdom to know what to do and we cry out to God to provide that wisdom.

The Serenity Prayer is a wonderful tool in marriage. Throughout the prayer we see an admission of humility in marriage, an acknowledgement that apart from God's help we can't manage control in our marriage and that we need God's wisdom and help to be married and at peace.

Robbie:

It wasn't until I joined a Celebrate Recovery group that I discovered the "rest of the story" as Paul Harvey would put it.

The Serenity Prayer written by Reinhold Niebuhr is not comprised of just the famous first three lines:

> *God, grant me the serenity to accept the things I cannot change,*
> *The courage to change the things I can,*
> *And the wisdom to know the difference,*

But it goes on:

> *Living one day at a time,*
> *Enjoying one moment at a time,*

Accepting hardship as a pathway to peace,
Taking, as Jesus did,
This sinful world as it is,
Not as I would have it,
Trusting that You will make all things right,
If I surrender to Your will,
So that I may be reasonably happy in this life,
And supremely happy with You forever in the next.
Amen.

My favorite line is "Accepting hardship as a pathway to peace…" Giving up control is difficult and it leads to emotional hardship as well as other kinds of hardships. But ultimately, giving up control leads to the peace that passes understanding (Philippians 4:7) that only God can give.

Chapter Twenty-three

Habit #8 – Ignite the Individuality in Your Spouse

Be who you are and say what you feel, because those who mind don't matter, and those who matter don't mind.

—Bernard M. Baruch[63]

Shedding Codependency

Robbie:

I am not fond of the word codependent. It sounds too much like a buzz word for crazy. So when I heard the word over and over when I joined Betty's therapy group, I cringed every time. I was not codependent, whatever that meant.

However, it turned out I was a walking case of codependency. To be codependent is to depend on someone else for your identity. As the hard shell of denial began to crack around my heart, I discovered that a huge part of my identity was tied to John.

He loved me – ergo, my identity was a loved woman.

He was a Godly man – (I made sure folks thought that) – ergo, my identity was a wife in a Godly marriage.

The reverse – the truth – was accurate also.

John had a secret addiction – ergo, my identity was a secret bearer.

John played at church – ergo, my identity was to make sure folks thought he was good at it.

When Betty asked me to list five things I did for myself, and I couldn't, it was the beginning of the end of my codependency. I began to see that before John I was a valuable, independent loved woman of Jesus who lost herself in the desperate need to be loved and married. After John I became a secret-bearing public relations woman, afraid people would know the truth. This realization starting me peeling myself from John – the un-velcroing process.

During our counseling I discovered that at the heart of my codependency problems were the expectations I brought into our marriage. I expected that John would meet my needs. Isn't a husband supposed to do that?

Wedding Day Expectations Must Die

I believed that all my insecurity about my weight and worthiness would end when I got married. I expected to live in a home filled with Godliness and fun. In fact, our home would be a little missionary home and John would be the head missionary. I expected five sons, in fact I pictured a little league infield, all populated by my boys. Family life would be a combination of the Waltons, the Bradys and the folks from Little House on the Prairie. I expected that John would feel like I did about life in general. I didn't expect perfection, at lease not from him, but I was extremely confident in my ability to be an almost-perfect wife and mom. Our marriage would be a beacon of fulfillment that every other couple would want.

John:

I expected that Robbie's fears and concerns about rejection would end. I expected peace in our home. I expected that I wouldn't have to feel guilty or ashamed about our physical relationship. I assumed that once we were married and having sex, my addiction would be more controlled. I expected that we would easily come to thinking and feeling similarly about household responsibilities and money – it would be easy.

Robbie:

We both had to come to terms with our expectations dying. It's like you marry one person and you tie all these expectations to that one person based on your dating relationship. But when you are married and you really see the other person for who they truly are, you resist letting go of those wedding day expectations. In order for marriage to work, we must each fully *accept* our spouse exactly like they are. Often, this means choosing to put to death those wedding-day dreams.

John:

This is not a bad thing. It is not "settling". It is an honest effort to continue to fall in love with the person you are living with, not just the person you thought they would be. For Robbie and me, ditching these expectations became more urgently needed because of the abrupt interruption to our marriage, i.e. Robbie leaving me. As difficult a year as it was to lay down our expectations and redefine our marriage, it was also rewarding because it turned into a genuine I-see-you and I-love-you-as-you-are kind of relationship.

Un-Velcroing

Robbie:

Going to separate therapy groups was our first step to the un-velcroing process. He went to work with a group of guys I didn't know and I worked on myself in the presence of women he didn't know. We both discovered that we *needed* time apart and I'm not just talking about two separate rooms in our house. We both needed to leave and enjoy the world and our friends without our spouse.

Some of you may be saying, "Of course." But John and I built our marriage on being together most of the time and with the duffel bag of insecurity I lugged around and the backpack of addiction he always had with him, we settled into an enmeshed unhealthy pattern.

So I looked at myself and decided what I wanted to do to nurture my heart, apart from John. I began writing in earnest away from our home. I began to make a point of having girl time just for the sake of being with my friends.

John:

I discovered that I enjoyed being with men. I wasn't afraid of them seeing the real me, like before. I began to just be me. For the first years of my recovery, I spent time with other men addicts, discovering what that meant. I also found a job, for the first time in my life, where I wasn't acting out. A consequence of my addiction was my employment. I was either unemployed or underemployed for much of our marriage. This was my first job in corporate America and the first time since I was in the Navy where my boss had a boss. The routine of a regular schedule and responsibilities had a very positive impact on my recovery and having a regular paycheck took a great deal of pressure off our budget. Thankfully, I did well and was promoted. In less than two years it was possible for Robbie to leave teaching and be home with Noah.

Robbie:

I remember John calling me while he was commuting to work. He'd been working at this company for two months.

"Something just occurred to me." He said.

"What's that?" I asked.

"This is how responsible people live. Wow."

That moment taught me a lot about how different John's perspective was as a sober man.

John:

Robbie wasn't a direct part of my recovery experience or my work life. We both began to live as individuals and it made us a better couple. Beyond work and recovery, we started to learn how to have parts of our lives apart. I'm not talking about having separate lives; we were still married and committed to each other and growing closer to one another. We simply stopped requiring the other to meet all our needs and make us the center of their world.

The Social Aspect

Robbie:

Another aspect of igniting your spouse's individuality is the social aspect. I am an extrovert; John is an introvert. Yet, many times I have expected him to meet my extravert needs and vice versa. It doesn't work and the expectation can lead to resentment, quiet fury or burning of clothes. (Well, not quite)

John and I have had to face this head on and deal with it. I did not marry a male version of me and I thank God for that. But I have experienced disappointment that John isn't me. For example, I love to go out and be with people. John can tolerate to be with approximately two to six people for approximately two-three hours. When he does go to a party, he does not enjoy it as much as I do, unless he sits with another introvert and they talk quietly.

I don't understand it. My father taught me a great deal about marriage when he used the phrase, "Viva la difference!" That is the attitude I need to take and sometimes it is difficult. I like fireworks and the fourth of July. John does not like crowds. I like going to movies often. John doesn't go often because he prefers to wait for the video so he can enjoy it in the living room.

Of course, it works both ways. John loves riding his motorcycle and has asked me to think about getting one to join him. I will only do this if they invent a motorcycle that acts and looks exactly like a car. John enjoys long drives. I do not, unless we are going to a specific place. John loves going to open houses and exploring homes. To me, it is a waste of time unless you have the gazillion dollars you need to buy it.

Viva la difference!

It took a while, but John and I have learned. I cannot meet most of John's social needs and he cannot meet mine. So we take care of our own hearts and nurture ourselves in this area when needed. I go to movies alone or with friends. John loves to motorcycle in the mountains by himself or with a few friends. I married a homebody and I have learned that being at home with John is wonderful. John married an extravert and he has learned that going out with me can be a blast. Just not all the time.

Motorcycles

When I was twelve, I fell off a motorcycle with my brother. Ever since, I have been extremely anti-motorcycle. My brother loves them and when John and I visited Phil and Lory early in our marriage, Phil asked John if he wanted to take a ride. I jumped in vehemently and said, "No! John will never ride a motorcycle." When I think of that instance, I cringe. So full of fear and control.

By our eleventh year of marriage, the Lord had grown me in courage and in trust. We'd moved to Denver and were settling into our lives. Phil and Lory happened to live twenty minutes away from us. One beautiful day John and I were in the car and he said, "I've been thinking about getting a motorcycle."

My heart did a double somersault with a twist. In my mind, I saw John on the side of the road, bleeding and barely breathing because of a horrible accident. But God had been walking me through a major growth spurt in my life in which I trusted Him, not my vain imaginations born of fear.

I quietly responded, "Okay, go for it." Inside my body, I was still doing mental gymnastics with all sorts of falls and injuries.

John got a motorcycle and developed his passion. One day in our thirteenth year, John left on a Sunday morning for a nice two-hour ride. He came back to our home a month later, having been in the hospital and rehab after a horrific accident. A traumatic brain injury changed our lives. In the hospital, I was instructed to get ready for a completely different John. When he woke up after a couple of days, I noticed his anger. He thrashed around and the people in the ICU put restraints on his arms and legs. It was a horrible time.

But God…

I love that phrase. But God in His mercy and grace, began working in John's brain and three months after his accident, our wonderful Physician healed John completely. During the rehab time, John said to me, "I want to ride again, Robbie." I thought he might change his mind later since his mind was changed.

But even after his cognitive abilities came back in full force, he was still insistent. "I want to ride again."

When God asked me to allow Him to be in charge of my husband, I said yes. But when my husband wanted to get back on a death machine, I found it difficult to not jump back in the old pattern.

"You will never ride a motorcycle again, John!" I didn't say this and I am glad. Instead, "John, go ahead. I will not live my life in fear." And I meant it. How could I cage my husband's wild heart? It would be trying to make my husband a carbon copy of myself. But I did add, "In order for me to have no reservations, I would like you to always have great life insurance."

I'm not stupid.

Quitting my Job

I trusted God with my husband's future. John did the same for me. My twentieth year of teaching began with a series of health problems and discontent. About that time, John got a raise at his job. I asked him if I could stay home. Noah was in first grade and I wanted to be there when he got home from school, not at a drama rehearsal or an after school meeting. We'd talked about me staying home in the past, but it was always a very short conversation. Both of us knew that economically, it would be ridiculous for me to not work.

John:

The transition to one income and that income coming from me was quite a shock to my system. In my addiction (so my entire adult life) I had never been able to stay in a job that had the ability to support a family, so I was always living paycheck to paycheck with too much debt and in the poorer parts of town. This had a negative impact on my first marriage as well and was upsetting to my father-in-law who paid for a car and provided numerous gifts to keep his daughter from living below the poverty line.

Now for the first time I had a real job with real benefits beyond medical. When Robbie was struggling at work and wanted to leave teaching, my initial reaction was fear. It was great having the income and structure at my job and I knew they liked me and my work. My concern was the pressure of everything relying on me. Even though I had been in recovery and sober for over two years, I was still hearing the voice of my old fears. From my father wound I still heard "Nothing I bring to any situation is true." The old messages of shame still whispered "If they knew the truth about me they would reject me." And "I am uniquely evil and beyond redemption." Most of the time I could dismiss those messages as being lies and move on to do the next right thing in my recovery, marriage and life. But the added pressure of being the single provider for our financial future brought all those fears and lies back to the forefront.

As I was struggling with these fears, I decided to treat it like any other issue in recovery and take it to trusted friends and God. After coming to peace with it, I realized that I owed Robbie an amends for the financial pressure I had placed on her and part of that amends was to "play the man" and accept that my shoulders were broad enough for this load. For the past ten years this has been the way we live.

Cheering for your Spouse's Individuality

Robbie:

To ignite the individuality in your spouse is to allow them to grow into what God wants them to be. This requires each of us to be cheerleaders for the other. As I un-velcroed myself from John, I discovered my heart's passion was to write and speak. In order for that to happen, John stood up and took on the financial responsibility. He compromised and led my cheering section.

As John has grown into his own man, I have had to kill those controlling instincts and cheer him on in the pursuits he loves. I don't complain when he takes a trip on his motorcycle or when he spends time with his guy friends, because I know his heart needs that time. John does the same for me.

John and I celebrate each other's differences instead of fighting them. As we've made these steps, our marriage has flourished. We are one flesh made from two independent souls.

5th Overarching Principle

When You Married, God had a Plan for You as a Couple. Live in it!

You were made by God and for God and until you understand that, life will never make sense.
—Rick Warren[64]

Chapter Twenty-Four

Habit #9 – Team up for God's Purposes

Many marriages would be better if the husband and the wife clearly understood that they are on the same side.
—Zig Ziglar[65]

Robbie:

When we got married, I was clear that our purpose was to obey what God told us to do. God would tell me and I would tell John. A perfect plan.

It didn't quite work that way. So my purpose morphed into making sure everyone thought we were great Christians. Then I left John and we had a life-changing year of reconciliation. After that year, my purpose became to write and speak for Jesus.

I didn't know it, but God had even more for us. Much more.

What's in a Name?

John:

Often in the Bible, God will give a person a new name that signifies a change in their life and tells them how God sees them. Abram became Abraham, Sari became Sarah, Jacob became Israel, Simon became Peter and John and James became known as the Sons of Thunder (coolest name ever). God promises us a new name when we meet Christ face to face. "Whoever has ears, let them hear what the Spirit says to the churches. To the one who is victorious, I will give some of the hidden manna. I will also give that person a white stone with a new name written on it, known only to the one who receives it" (Revelations 2:17).

After my motorcycle accident and the rehab process, I returned to work and one of my coworkers gave me a new name. They referred to it as my Indian Name, like *Dances with Wolves* and while it does not carry the same significance as God giving you a new name it was funny. My new name was *One with Pavement*. When I returned to riding, I even considered having that name made into a patch for my jacket.

In my addiction, I carried names or identities that were driven by shame. Names that led me to believe I would never amount to anything. In fact, at one point after being removed from ministry because of my acting out, I made a deal with God that I would never be involved with ministry again. My name, although I never said this aloud, was *Minister No More*.

So I settled into my life in recovery, corporate America and my improving marriage. It was all going very well and it seemed we were living a blessed life. When we moved to Denver we bought a home and for the first time in my life I wasn't living in a rental.

The move to Denver ignited Robbie's writing and speaking and we were living the life we were meant to live. The motorcycle accident shook up that life. After I fully recovered, I decided to take a Weekend Alone with God or what we call a WAWG.

Robbie's brother, Phil Floyd, is the founder of *Caleb's Heart Ministry* and Phil and this ministry has had a profound effect on both Robbie and me.[66] Part of what Caleb's Heart does is teach people how to spend time alone with God by taking them on a WAAWG. (Weekend Almost Alone with God when it's a group.) WAAWGS are not like normal retreats. No speaker speaks. The goal is to teach participants how to be alone with God for extended periods of time. Like hours at a time. Both Robbie and I have been on those group weekends and they have changed how we communicate with God and how we make decisions. We now regularly take individual weekends to be alone with God.

On the WAWG I took after my motorcycle accident, God said something very specific to me. It wasn't audible but I knew it was Him. He said, *You know the deal we have where you will never be involved in ministry again? I was never part of that deal.* I was shocked and assumed He had specific directions for me but that was all He said.

It wasn't until a few years later on a group WAAWG with my band of brothers, eight other men who also love Jesus, where God spoke to me again on the subject. We all decided to bring the same question to God on the WAAWG, "What is my new name?" The name God told me was *Pastor*. It was clear to me He was not calling me to that "job" but to the role of a shepherd, one who cares for the sheep.

Wolves, Sheep and Sheepdogs

In the book *On Combat*, Lt. Colonel David Grossman tells a story where he describes society using the metaphor of wolves, sheep and sheepdogs.[67] His words have influenced my understanding of my addiction and recovery.

In short, most people are like sheep in that they would never harm or kill another except in an accident or under extreme provocation. Unfortunately, there are wolves who prey on the sheep. In my addiction, I would objectify others for my own pleasure and satisfaction; I became a wolf and the sheep were not safe around me. Many times I would pretend to be safe so I was a wolf in sheep's clothing. That was never truer than when I was in a ministry role.

At that WAAWG, God gave me the new name *Pastor*. As I sat and prayed and listened, I understood it to mean the third part of the metaphor from Grossman's story. I was to live as a sheepdog. Sheepdogs are very much like wolves, with their long legs and sharp fangs and they clearly have the ability to kill sheep; but instead they protect the sheep from the wolves. I came to understand the difference between wolves and sheepdogs to be as simple as this:

Wolves only serve their appetite and the desires of the pack.

Sheepdogs serve the shepherd.

It was necessary that rather than denying or suppressing my wolf-like tendencies, I take them to the cross and submit them to my King Jesus and in His hands become a new creature. In becoming a sheepdog, I would care for, rather than prey on, the sheep.

On another WAAWG God spoke to me again and I knew I was to start *Tin Men Ministries*. The name is from the *Wizard of Oz* and refers to the problem of the Tin Man living without a heart. Too many Christian men live life stuck in their heads and don't trust or are not able to live from their hearts. The goal of this ministry was to encourage men to trust God with their hearts.

Two years later God had me return to school and become a counselor and life coach and the ministry name changed to *Tin Men Counseling*. There is power in a name and power in the identity we hold and believe about ourselves. My life is completely different now because of the new name God gave me.

Robbie:

Let me jump in here and say it is a humbling truth to admit you married a wolf. But I did. I chose him. In my desperation, I chose someone without taking the time to really get to know his heart. But God, in His grace and mercy, turned my husband into a sheepdog. Being married to a sheepdog is a wonderful honor.

God has changed my name/identity over the years from *Unworthy because She is Overweight* to *Beloved just as She is*. When I think of the work He has done in my life, I relate to Hannah Hurnard's main character in the book *Hinds Feet on High Places*.[68] She begins the book as *Much Afraid* and ends with the name *Grace and Glory*.

A Purpose Together

John:

We had placed a high priority on serving God and living in our calling. That is a great thing and every Christian would benefit from considering changes in his life to move in the direction of living out God's calling. So what we were doing was good for us and good for our marriage. The problem or "unintended consequence" was that our ministry lives were completely separate and had no overlap.

When we considered sharing our story in this book, it became apparent that the book was going to put us in front of couples who are in pain and struggling to find hope for their marriages. We realized that the understanding of our calling and ministry was too narrow and that we needed to repent of our small vision and faith and go to God and ask Him to show us His larger vision for our lives and marriage.

These questions took us to the birth of *Caught in His Arms Ministry*.

God's purpose for our marriage right now is to encourage married couples to put God in the center of their relationship and to deal with addiction, if it is a part of the marriage, head on. But of course, every marriage is unique and has a unique purpose. The problem that we come across often is most couples don't even consider their purpose. They marry because of love/lust. Once the "I dos" are said the mindset of the newlyweds is usually about adjusting to each other and learning how to love consistently. It's almost survival mode at times. Purpose is usually not a big consideration.

If the marriage is blessed by children, the purpose is obvious. Raise the children in the best way possible. Incorporating God into the lives of your babies is vital. Also, surviving the child rearing years is a great goal.

But what about later in life when your children begin to get self-sufficient? This is a great time to once again, consider your purpose as a couple. What does God have in mind for you, not only as individuals, but as a twosome team? It is also great preparation for the empty nest stage.

The Three P's to Purpose

To begin finding your purpose as a couple, let us recommend a method using three P's: Prayer, Personality and Patience.

Prayer

As we already discussed in a previous holy habit it is critical that you and your spouse pray together both with and for each other. What we are recommending now is that you include in your prayers the request that God lead you to His purpose for you as a couple. As He does, He may reveal the unique place in His kingdom that He has set aside just for the two of you. Maybe your purpose is to be an encouragement to your pastor or ministry leaders rather than start a ministry or plant a church. Maybe God has given you both a burden and a desire to lead or help in an area in your church. As you pray, pay attention to what He brings to mind and discuss it with each other.

Personality

Psalm 37:4 tells us to "Delight in the Lord and He will give us the desires of our hearts." I believe when God speaks to us about our purpose it will be a perfect fit for our hearts, temperaments and personality. I hear people say they are afraid of hearing from God about purpose because they are sure it will mean needing to move to Africa to become missionaries. Clearly God calls people to be missionaries, but they are people whose hearts are already moved by the needs of people in far off lands.

If your passion is for better education and schools, your purpose is more likely to get involved with the PTA than to move to Africa. God knows your heart; He did, after all, give it to you in the first place. Trust me, when God leads you in a direction it will seem as natural as taking your next breath. Robbie and I were already actively teaching and caring for people as individuals so our purpose as a couple naturally aligned with the calling of God to teach and help couples.

Patience

Discovering your purpose as a couple can and will take time. A motorcycle trip I recently took was part of discovering our purpose. I rode five thousand miles across twenty states. Two of the ways I best relate to and have time with God are solitude and worship music. During that trip I had nine days alone with very little face to face interaction and when I rode I listened to audio books and worship music. Spending time with Jesus, asking about life and listening to Him helped me realize that He wanted me to take the financial risk of full time ministry rather than look for another corporate job when my job ended. Coming home with that kind of announcement was surprising to say the least. Robbie responded by a) screaming and then b) taking both a group WAAWG and a solo WAWG where God confirmed my decision to her.

Again your purpose as a couple does not need to be a ministry and doesn't need to mean quitting your job. We've met couples who felt drawn to take a once a year mission trip. Another couple we know feel deeply that their mission is to fund other ministries. Other possibilities for the purpose God might have for your marriage:

Parenting – Especially if you have little ones, raising your children according to God's leading is your purpose as a couple.

Athletics - leading the sports leagues in your area as a couple

Social Justice - protesting, leading in political rallies, initiating voting registrations and working voting districts

Encouragement - writing cards of encouragement, taking people to dinner just to encourage them and say job well done

Prayer - leading a prayer team or teaching others to pray

Hospitality - hosting a Bible study or regularly inviting people over to lunch or dinner

Service - as a couple regularly help in community projects

Volunteering - blood drives, school functions, church events

Youth - dedicate your home to be a place for your neighborhood youth to feel welcomed

Kids - Sunday school volunteers or Vacation Bible School volunteers

Habitat for Humanity - building together a home that will help others

Mentors – we at *Caught in His Arms* are always looking for couples to help younger couples. We also look for couples who have recovery experience.

Robbie:

A few years ago, John and I read a great book titled *Sacred Pathways* by Gary Thomas.[69] In it, Thomas teaches believers to embrace the unique way that you interact with God. It's not always a quiet time or singing. Gary describes nine different ways Christians relate to Christ. As a couple, this book helped John and I begin talking about the ways we relate to God. Our discussions laid a foundation to find our purpose as a couple.

When we married, my happiness was the sole objective. John's personal goals put him in the center of the marriage, too. Like many couples, the ultimate purpose for marriage was to *make me happy*.

Marriage can be so much more fulfilling. Discovering that God made me for a definite purpose is freeing. Finding out God also had something wonderful in mind when John and I got married has catapulted our relationship to one that is beyond personal happiness. It is about changing the world, one conversation at a time and one moment of service at a time. Don't miss this incredible opportunity for your marriage. Begin now to explore your purpose as a couple.

Chapter Twenty-five

Habit #10 –
Sow Laughter and Reap Joy!

He who laughs…lasts.
—Erma Bombeck[70]

Robbie:

It's early morning and John and I are sitting on our balcony, gently swaying on our swing. No one is speaking. I'm drinking coffee, trying to wake up and John, not a caffeine fan, is looking out at the sky, contemplating. Content.

Five minutes later.

Our eyes are both flooded with moisture and we are laughing loudly. Why? Somehow in the maze of conversation that is marriage we began wondering what it would be like if Billy Bob Thornton was to play Solomon as the main character in *Sling Blade*.[71]

"Uhhh-huuuhhh. I sure like them wisdom. Got some fried taters and mustard with 'em?"

Ridiculous but funny.

John and I have found the formula for laughter in our marriage. If I could write it out for you I would. But I can't. It's different for each couple. But it is so important to keep in your home, like a fire extinguisher or an extra set of keys.

When you discover it, this formula should be used often. Laughter is vital. When laughter bubbles up in a home, the giggles and guffaws form little circles that rise up to the ceiling and pop open. Joy floats down and covers everything.

When there is laughter, perspective is easier to find when arguments occur.

When there is laughter, the happiness it produces is like a bonding glue, sticking your souls closer together.

When there is laughter, joy grows.

The other day I took to Facebook and I asked this question: When is the last time you laughed with your spouse and why?

The answers were wonderful and provide a clue as to finding the formula for you and your spouse:

1. *We laughed during the Minions movie, because it was funny.*
2. *Just last night we laughed while watching our favorite show together.*

Watching TV shows and movies can often spur on laughter and bonding. Seeing something together is a shared experience and can often lead to a reoccurring joke in your family.

3. *Bodily functions.*
4. *This morning we laughed about flatulence.*

Hey, if you both love this kind of humor, go for it. Cultivate it. Well…maybe not so much.

5. *Lying in bed reminiscing about when we first started dating.*
6. *We laugh all the time. One of our funnies that continue to make us smile is remembering our first date. We played tackle football in a goose poop covered field before a college class. We both attended without showering.*

Laughter can so easily be evoked in a marriage with "Remember when?" Memories are sometimes gift bags of giggles just waiting to be opened.

7. *I think I know the lyrics to songs and apparently have no clue. My husband was singing in his best Captain Feathersword voice along with the Wiggles for the kids.*

    I said, 'That's what they say?'

    He said, 'Yes, what did you think it said?'

    I had sung the wrong lyrics for ten years. They say 'from every wharf and pier' and I thought it was 'from every wombat here'. Needless to say, we cried in laughter when he sang my version.
8. *Today. I had an eye exam and my husband had to lead me out to the car afterward. So funny! We laugh together every single day. 41 years plus.*

It's vital to be able to laugh at yourself with your partner and vice versa. Not in a mean or dishonoring way, of course.

9. *We laughed yesterday in church (before the service started) because my husband kept scooting closer and closer to me. Each time I moved over a little bit (needing some space, thank you very much) he'd move also. We started laughing.*
10. *We actually tend to laugh during fights. We try to keep a straight face and stay "mad" but inevitably one of us will do something funny and then it's all over. We still have to work through our stuff, but it's such a great way to lighten the mood a bit and not take ourselves so seriously.*

Laughter is like water in the dry desert of hard dirt. It brings refreshment and makes the foundation of your marriage more pliable. Laughter smooths out difficult moments and eases tension. Every marriage needs laughter.

California's Loma Linda University did a study that showed laughter improves recall and lowers stress.[72] Other studies have also shown the wide-ranging health benefits of laughter. A Vanderbilt University study estimated that just 10-15 minutes of laughter a day can burn up to 40 calories.[73] Meanwhile, the American Heart Association has proven that humor and heart health are connected.[74]

"A cheerful heart is good medicine, but a crushed spirit dries up the bones" (Proverbs 17:22).

It's proven. So knowing that laughter can result in happiness and health, why not make a conscious decision to inject laughter into your marriage?

John:

Robbie is active on social media and has several friends on Facebook. A few years ago, Robbie began to jot down short conversations we'd have that ended in laughter. Robbie calls them Moments in a Marriage. She received dozens of requests to put them in a book. So working with an artist friend and his wife, Matthew and Kimbra Birchler, we are creating another book with a significantly lighter mood than *Caught* called *Moments in a Marriage*.

Here's a couple of examples:

Moments in a Marriage:

(While watching TV, a commercial comes on for a new show about an elite team of geniuses.)

Me: "Elite team of Geniuses?" Yet they never call me.

John: Sigh.

Me: I know, right?

John: I had to change my number. I'm so over the team thing.

Moments in a Marriage:

(John takes me to breakfast at Gunther Toody's:)

John: You are much prettier than Marilyn.

Me: You are such a smooth talker, John.

John: So I'm not better looking than Elvis?

Me: Um...of course you are.

John: So we agree. We are much better looking than dead people.

In Psalm 126, the writer talks about a people rescued from captivity, probably Babylon. A marriage in trouble rescued from crisis can claim this Psalm. We love Psalm 126:2 because it tells of what God has done for Robbie and me. "Our mouths were filled with laughter, our tongues with songs of joy. Then it was said among the nations, 'The LORD has done great things for them.'"

Chapter Twenty-Six

The Redemption of a Marriage

The marvelous richness of human experience would lose something of rewarding joy if there were no limitations to overcome. The hilltop hour would not be half so wonderful if there were no dark valleys to traverse.

—Helen Keller[75]

God Redeems Us – We Don't Redeem Us

John:

We are convinced that if you add the ten holy habits to your marriage you will have greater intimacy, joy and satisfaction in your marriage. We know this from our own experience and from the feedback of many couples. It is universal: if you do the work, the results follow. However, these habits, this book, nor any other help we can offer is the redeemer of your marriage. We are not the point. Jesus is the point.

Marriage is a deeply spiritual thing and was created by God to be the representation of the kind of intimacy He wants between us and Him. As with all matters of faith, we walk in dynamic tension between walking in the trust of God and doing good that pleases God. The ten holy habits that we live and have recommended in this book clearly fall into the category of doing good works. There is a place for that in the faith walk of every Christian and in every Christian marriage. If we didn't believe that, we would have never written this book.

But—doing good works can never become the point.

These habits, this book, our marriage and yours must first and foremost rely on God's grace, God's love and God's redemption are made available to you and me through the life, death, burial and resurrection of Jesus. No other name under heaven or on earth can save your marriage. All of this starts with Jesus and ends with Jesus. We do the good works, not to earn His love or favor, but instead as a response to His love and favor.

Ephesians 2:10 "For we are God's handiwork, created in Christ Jesus to do good works, which God prepared in advance for us to do."

I believe that living well in our marriages is part of the good works that God prepared in advance for us to do. The ten holy habits are a way to honor God and to honor and love your spouse. We want to again make it clear that it is God and not our good works that redeem us. We do the work in response to His love and grace, never to qualify for it by being good enough.

The Rewards of a Redeemed Marriage

Robbie:

The rewards of a redeemed marriage are always multiplying in our lives. Because God rescued us, our son lives in a home where pornography is not allowed to exist. We take it seriously and consider it an evil that causes serious damage. When it sneaks in, we kick it out. Noah's life will be fuller and richer because we have made this choice that began with God's redemption.

I do not live with the kind of insecurity that marriage to a sex addict can grow. One of the lies that pornography tells women is that they must look a certain way to be worthy of love. God has redeemed my heart and mind from this type of thinking. I used to live the lie that says "I will be able to do anything once I lose weight". Now I live the truth "I can do all things *right now* through Christ who strengthens me".

Redemption has caused our marriage to be secret-free. In our first years, we lived as if a wife and a husband *needed* to keep secrets to have a good marriage. God has rescued us from that lie.

Because our marriage is a redeemed one, we know that work is vital to keeping our marriage fun and fulfilling. Maintenance of our marriage means we choose selflessness and we choose going first, even when it feels exhausting. The rewards show up in those moments where John shoots me that smile that I know is only for me. Or those moments when we shout "Family hug!" and even our sixteen-year-old comes over to join in. The work is worth it.

I like to think of the specific moments God has given John and I to remind us that He rescued us:

When we watch TV, we try to DVR everything when possible so we can fast forward through the commercials. If we are watching it live, John or I usually hold the remote. If something questionable comes on, like a lingerie ad, John turns away and hits fast forward. If I am there, John looks away and I hit fast forward. This is an automatic response for John and he has taught Noah to do the same thing, be it in our living room or a movie theater. Once I was away and Noah was having some guys over. John and the teens watched some movie that had a scene where a young lady took off her shirt to reveal just her bra. When that happened, John looked at Noah and Noah looked at him automatically.

The other guys talked about how hot she was, but John and Noah just smiled knowingly at each other. We know Noah will have to stand on his own and face this battle by himself, but for him to not even hesitate to look away, even in front of his friends, was a wonderful moment for John and me.

God's redemption is not just for us, but for Noah, too.

We'd been married for a couple of years when we went to a dinner theatre with a group of friends. Our waitress, who was also a cast member, took delight in flirting with my husband and John enjoyed every moment and returned the audacious flirting with some of his own. I was humiliated. In our marriage now, John takes delight it flirting with me in front of anyone and everyone and won't allow a waitress or another woman to have one moment of his attention. No matter where we are, I know John chooses me over anyone else in the room.

This is redemption.

Once in the early years, I opened up the glove box of our car and found two pornographic videos. John was driving and we had this horrible awkward five minutes of silence. I was ashamed and angry and hurt. I ended the silence with a rant meant to shame him into being a better Christian husband. (Of course, it didn't work) After that I often looked in the glove box, ready to be angry.

After John got sober, I didn't want to look in the glove box, frightened that it would mean he'd slipped or worse, was lying to me. But one day, about six years into his sobriety, I was looking for something and didn't think before opening up the glove box. I saw a book. It was "The Love Dare" based on the movie *Fireproof*.[76] The book is a 40-day challenge to do little things for your spouse, little acts of love. I realized John had been doing sweet things for me out of that book. In secret, he was addicted to pornography. Now, his only secret was to surprise me with acts of love.

That's redemption.

Doug was John's counselor and our marriage counselor the first year of his sobriety. John respects this man deeply, as do I. When John was thinking about going back to school to be a counselor he sought Doug's counsel. Doug's exact words were "It's about time."

That is redemption for my man's heart.

Our story is about a little boy in California who started looking at pornography when he was eight years old. He dreamed of being loved for exactly who he was. But the enemy used pornography to lie to him and tell him that the women in those magazines and movies proved their love to him by being willing to show themselves to him. The most natural response for a woman when she senses someone seeing her undressed is to cover herself. In pornography, the enemy propagates the lie that a woman doesn't cover herself because she is relieved it's someone worthy – it's you. John saw those women as the answer to being fully and completely loved. They didn't demand anything; they just accepted him. The insidious plan of the enemy launches every time anyone looks at porn, young or old, male or female.

Our story is also the story of a little girl in Texas who saw pornography for the first time when she was eight years old. She was a little girl who wanted to be loved and accepted. The enemy attacked her soul when she saw that picture. The arrow in her heart read – you must look like this woman to be worthy of love. Those words were reinforced by a silly little third grader who told her she would get a boyfriend when she lost weight. The little girl grew up and dreamed of being loved and rescued by a Godly man – hopefully a pastor. One who, by marrying and loving her, would prove to her she was indeed worthy.

The little girl met the little boy.

It was a train wreck of a marriage.

BUT GOD...

God taught the little boy that he was a man of worth and courage and he was loved.

God taught the little girl that she was a woman of worth and courage and she was loved.

God redeemed that man and that woman. And He redeemed their marriage.

All we were ever looking for, now we have. Not because of anything we could ever do, but because of a God who loves to redeem His children.

If you are reading this, please know there is hope and redemption available to you right now. Ask the Father to begin a work in your life and the life of your mate.

Happily-ever-after is just in fairy tales. Redemption is real and available for all of us. With it, comes a rich abundant life. May our Lord begin in you that work of abundant redemption.

"The thief comes only to steal and kill and destroy; I have come that they may have life, and have it to the full" (John 10:10).

Your Free *Caught* Workbook Is Waiting for You

Get your free workbook to help you on your journey. You've purchased the book and you're ready to take action. This free workbook will help you with your journey and keep you on your path to success.

All you have to do is go to
www.caughtinhisarms.com/caughtworkbook/
to get your free workbook today.

Once there, put your name and email address in the spaces provided and then click the button to download your workbook immediately.

It's that easy!

Don't Wait! Get Your Free Workbook Right Now!

Caught – Next Steps

Thank you for reading *Caught*. It is our hope that our story has helped your marriage. When dealing with a topic as vast and important as marriage, no single book can answer every question or concern so we would like to offer additional help as follows:

Day Long Marriage Seminar
We are available to come to your church or community and present the Ten Holy Habits in an interactive presentation.

Weekend Marriage Conference
Like the day long seminars, the weekend conference focuses on the Ten Holy Habits allowing for additional time for activities to make the habits your own.

Short Presentations
We are available for speaking on marriage or addiction, also.

To contact us about coming to your church or community please visit www.caughtinhisarms.com/contact

Marriage Blog
We offer additional help and marriage tips in the form of a marriage blog. Please visit our blog and subscribe at www.caughtinhisarms.com/blog/

Marriage and Relationship Coaching
John and Robbie are Christian Life Coaches with a certificate in Marriage Coaching from the American Associations of Christian Counselors. We offer coaching services anywhere by phone or in person if you live in the Denver area. We can also make appointments if we are in your area for a conference. To contact us about coaching please visit www.caughtinhisarms.com

Sexual Addiction and Trauma Counseling
John is a Certified Biblical counselor specializing in shame from past trauma, sin and addiction; he is also a registered psychotherapist in the state of Colorado. Counseling services are only available in Colorado due to the limitations imposed by the Colorado Department of Regulatory Agencies.

To contact John please visit http://www.tinmencounseling.com/contact/ and use the phone number and email address provided.

John also offers a weekly free email called Lessons from the Road to Recovery. You can sign up for this free no obligation service by visiting http://www.tinmencounseling.com/contact/ and leaving your name and email address on the site.

Moments in a Marriage

A book of cartoons to make you laugh. Actual moments from our marriage! For information about this upcoming book, go to www. caughtinhisarms.com

About the Authors:

John and Robbie Iobst have been married for 20 years. John is a registered psychotherapist and a Biblical Counselor. Together, Robbie and John are professional marriage coaches. Robbie has written 2 books, a devotional titled *Joy Dance* and a Colorado Independent Publishers Award winning novel, *Cecilia Jackson's Last Chance*. The Iobsts both speak at conferences and are marriage contributors to the nationally syndicated radio program Daybreak, USA as well as guests on several local and regional programs. John and Robbie have 3 daughters, 1 son, 4 grand girls and 2 dogs.

Resources

12 Step Fellowships for Sex Addiction
    Sex Addicts Anonymous - SAA https://saa-recovery.org/
    Sex and Love Addicts Anonymous - SLAA http://www.slaafws.org/
    Sexaholics Anonymous - SA https://www.sa.org/

Dr. Mark Laaser, M.Div., Ph.D., Founder/Director of Faithful & True
Treatment program provided by the top Christian experts in the sexual addiction field
www.faithfulandtrue.com

Mark Batterson
Pastor, National Community Church in Washington D. C.
www.markbatterson.com

Patrick Carnes
Gentle Path at The Meadows
www.gentlepathmeadows.com

Gary Chapman
Author and Speaker
www.5lovelanguages.com

John Elderidge
Ransomed Heart Ministries
www.ransomedheart.com

Bob Goff
Restore International
www.bobgoff.com

Mark Merrill
Family First
www.markmerrill.com

Dr. David Stoop
New Life
www.newlife.com

Gary Thomas
Author and Speaker
www.garythomas.com

The National Association of Marriage Enhancement
Phoenix, AZ
www.nameonline.net

Bibliography

1. Tolkien, J. R. R. The Two Towers; Being the Second Part of The Lord of the Rings. Boston: Houghton Mifflin, 1965.
2. Punchline. Directed by David Seltzer. Performed by Tom Hanks. Columbia Pictures, 1988. Film.
3. Bambi. Directed by David Hand. United States: Disney Enterprises, Inc., 1942. Film.
4. Mr. Holland's Opus. Directed by Stephen Herek. Performed by Richard Dreyfuss. Buena Vista Pictures, 1995. Film.
5. Page, Ken. "How Our Insecurities Can Reveal Our Deepest Gifts." Psychology Today. September 24, 2011. https://www.psychologytoday.com/blog/finding-love/201109/how-our-insecurities-can-reveal-our-deepest-gifts.
6. Eldredge, John. Wild at Heart: Discovering the Passionate Soul of a Man. Nashville, TN: T. Nelson, 2001.
7. Quote is sometimes attributed to Mark Twain, but no citation exists.

8. Lambert, Miranda, writer. Four the Record. RCA Nashville, 2011, CD. One line from "Mama's Broken Heart."

9. Www.thefreedictionary.com.

10. Balsan, Consuelo Vanderbilt. The Glitter and the Gold. New York: Harper, 1952. Winston Churchill to Lady Astor.

11. Jackson, Rob. "When Children View Pornography." Focus on the Family, 2004.

12. Collins, Mabel. Light on the Path; a Treatise Written for the Personal Use of Those Who Are Ignorant of the Eastern Wisdom and Who Desire to Enter within Its Influence. Covina, CA: Theosophical University Press, 1949.

13. White, Cindy. "Pornography Hijacks the Brain - Marriage Missions International." Marriage Missions International. October 31, 2011. Accessed March 07, 2016. http://marriagemissions.com/pornograp-hijacks-the-brain/.

14. It's a Wonderful Life. Directed by Frank Capra. Performed by Jimmy Stewart. New York: RKO Radio Pictures, 1946. DVD.

15. Thoreau, Henry David. Walden. Boston: J.R. Osgood, 1878.

16. Galsworthy, John. The Forsythe Sage - Awakening & To Let: "Beginnings Are Always Messy." 1907.

17. An Officer and a Gentleman. Directed by Taylor Hackford. United States: Paramount Pictures, 1982. Film.

18. Cocker, Joe, and Jennifer Warnes, writers. Up Where We Belong. Praise Hymn Soundtracks, 1982, CD.

19. Gray, Zach. "SOS: 5 Reasons Asking for Help Should Never Feel Embarrassing." Elite Daily SOS 5 Reasons Asking for Help Should Never Feel Embarrassing Comments. 2014. Accessed March 07, 2016. http://elitedaily.com/life/5-reasons-asking-help-good/838636/. Story quoted is from Anonymous

20. Fergusson, David. Scottish Proverbs. Edinburgh: Printed by Robert Bryson, and Are to Be Sold at His Shop at the Signe of Jonah, 1641.
21. Quote "God created man, but I could do better." Erma Bombeck
22. Quote - "Prayer does change things, all kinds of things. But the most important thing it changes is us." R.C Sproul
23. Quote – "Addiction is a forgetting disease, but I forgot that." Anonymous
24. Quote - "Nothing changes if nothing changes, and if I keep doing what I've always done, I'll keep getting what I've always got, and will keep feeling what I always felt." Anonymous
25. Quote – "Life is a succession of lessons which must be lived to be understood." Helen Keller
26. Carnes, Patrick, and Patrick Carnes. Out of the Shadows: Understanding Sexual Addiction. Center City, MN: Hazelden Information & Edu, 2001. Print.
27. Eldredge, John. Wild at Heart: Discovering the Passionate Soul of a Man. Nashville, TN: T. Nelson, 2001.
28. Hall, Mark and Herms, Bernie, writers. Thrive. AVT Tree Publishing (BMI) Artists Casting Crowns. 2014, CD. 2 lines from "Broken Together."
29. Abrams, J.J. "Lost." Lost. ABC. Television. Transcript. Caught in the Arms of a Loving God
30. Chinese Proverb.
31. Lutzer, Erwin W. The Truth about Same-sex Marriage: 6 Things You Need to Know about What's Really at Stake. Chicago: Moody, 2004. Print.
32. "The Beta Marriage: How Millennials Approach 'I Do'" Time. July 25, 2014. Accessed March 09, 2016. http://time.com/3024606/millennials-marriage-sex-relationships-hook-ups/.

33. "7 Ways to Shift Your Thinking about Marriage." Dave Willis. 26 Dec. 2014. Web. 08 Mar. 2016.

34. Goff, Bob. Love Does: Discover a Secretly Incredible Life in an Ordinary World. Nashville: Thomas Nelson, 2012. Print.

35. Alexie, Sherman. The Toughest Indian in the World. New York: Atlantic Monthly, 2000. Print.

36. Quote. "Many things I have tried to grasp and have lost. That which I have placed in God's hands I still have." Martin Luther

37. Www.vocabulary.com

38. Lamott, Anne. Help, Thanks, Wow: The Three Essential Prayers. New York: Riverhead, 2012. Print.

39. Merrill, Mark. "The 8 Benefits of Praying with Your Spouse." IMom. 2010. Web. 08 Mar. 2016.

40. Gallup Poll by The National Association of Marriage Enhancement, in Phoenix, Arizona 1997 (www.nameonline.net)

41. "The Couple That Prays Together." Dr. David Stoop. 6 Aug. 2012. Web. 08 Mar. 2016.

42. The Divorce Experience. http://assets.aarp.org/rgcenter/general/divorce.pdf May.2004.

43. Batterson, Mark. The Circle Maker: Praying Circles around Your Biggest Dreams and Greatest Fears. Grand Rapids, MI: Zondervan, 2011. Print.

44. "Tudie Rose." Tudie Rose. 2012. Web. 08 Mar. 2016.

45. Indiana Jones and the Raiders of the Lost Ark. Dir. Steven Spielberg. Paramount, 1981. Film.

46. Chapman, Gary D. Five Love Languages. SEND THE LIGHT DISTRIBUTION, 1995. Print.

47. A League of Their Own. Dir. Penny Marshall. Prod. Robert Greenhut. By Lowell Ganz. Perf. Tom Hanks, Geena Davis, and Madonna. Columbia Pictures, 1992.

48. Quote. "The difficult thing is that vulnerability is the first thing I look for in you and the last thing I'm willing to show you. In you, it's courage and daring. In me, it's weakness." Brene Brown

49. Vanauken, Sheldon. A Severe Mercy. Harper and Row. 1977. Print

50. Roloff, Jeremy. "Little People, Big World." Little People, Big World. Aug. 2013. Television. Transcript.

51. Roloff, Audrey. "Let's Beat the 50 Percent." http://www.aujpoj.com

52. Ibsen, Henrik. A Doll's House. Ghosts. New York: C. Scribner's Sons, 1906. Print.

53. Love Story. Dir. Arthur Hiller. Perf. Ryan O'Neal. Ken Films, 1970. Film.

54. Smith, William P. Loving Well: (even If You Haven't Been). Greensboro, NC: New Growth, 2012. Print.

55. Quote. "The tongue has no bones but is strong enough to break a heart." Anonymous

56. Quote. "Comparison is the thief of joy." Teddy Roosevelt

57. Quote. "If two people who love each other let a single instant wedge itself between them, it grows – it becomes a month, a year, a century; it becomes too late." Jean Giraudoux

58. Miller, Donald. A Million Miles in a Thousand Years: What I Learned While Editing My Life. Thomas Nelson, 2011. Print.

59. Quote. "You must do the thing you think you cannot do." Eleanor Roosevelt

60. Quote. "Men marry women with the hope they will never change. Women marry men with the hope they will change. Invariably they are both disappointed." Albert Einstein.

61. Quote. "God, grant me the serenity to accept the things I cannot change, the courage to change the things I can and the wisdom to know the difference." Reinhold Niebuhr

62. Owen, Mark, and Kevin Maurer. No Hero: The Evolution of a Navy SEAL. Dutton, 2014.

63. Quote. "Be who you are and say what you feel, because those who mind don't matter, and those who matter don't mind." Bernard M. Baruch

64. Warren, Richard. The Purpose-Driven Life: What on Earth Am I Here for? Grand Rapids, MI: Zondervan, 2002.

65. Quote. "Many marriages would be better if the husband and the wife clearly understood that they are on the same side." Zig Ziglar

66. Caleb's Hearts Ministries www.calebsheartministries.org

67. Grossman, Dave, and Loren W. Christensen. On Combat: The Psychology and Physiology of Deadly Conflict in War and in Peace. Millstadt, IL: Warrior Science Pub., 2008.

68. Hurnard, Hannah. Hinds' Feet on High Places. Wheaton, IL: Tyndale House, 1975. Print.

69. Thomas, Gary. Sacred Pathways: Discover Your Soul's Path to God. Grand Rapids, MI: Zondervan, 2000.

70. Bombeck, Erma. Forever, Erma. Missouri: Andrews and McMeel, 1996.

71. Sling Blade. Directed by Billy Bob. Thornton. 1996. Film.

72. Shah, Yagana. "New Study Proves That Laughter Really Is the Best Medicine." The Huffington Post. April 22, 2014. Accessed March 08, 2016. http://www.huffingtonpost.com/2014/04/22/laughter-and-memory_n_5192086.html.

73. "No Joke: Study Finds Laughing Can Burn Calories (06/10/05)." No Joke: Study Finds Laughing Can Burn Calories (06/10/05). June 10, 2005. Accessed March 08, 2016. http://www.mc.vanderbilt.edu:8080/reporter/index.html?ID=4030.

74. "Humor Helps Your Heart? How?" Humor Helps Your Heart? How? June 24, 2015. Accessed March 08, 2016. http://www.heart.org/HEARTORG/HealthyLiving/Humor-helps-your-heart-How_UCM_447039_Article.jsp#.Vt6Fs_krLIU.

75. Quote. "The marvelous richness of human experience would lose something of rewarding joy if there were no limitations to overcome. The hilltop hour would not be half so wonderful if there were no dark valleys to traverse." Helen Keller

76. Kendrick, Stephen, Alex Kendrick, and Lawrence Kimbrough. The Love Dare. Nashville, TN: B & H Publishing Group, 2008.